More Praise for *The Five Thieves of Happiness*

"The only things holding you back from complete peace of mind are mental, and this book shows you how to remove these barriers once and for all."
—**Brian Tracy, author of** *The Power of Self-Confidence*

"*Five Thieves* is a perfect complement to *Five Secrets*. Dr. Izzo gives us not only a pencil with which to sketch the good but now the eraser to rid the bad."
—**Dr. Geoff Smart, founder and Chairman, ghSMART, and coauthor of** *Who*

"In a world on the brink of either returning to the dark ages or entering the next great renaissance, John's book comes along to help us remember that happiness is available to us all, despite our circumstances, if we become present to the things that are keeping us from it and choose it for ourselves."
—**KoAnn Vikoren Skrzyniarz, founder and CEO, Sustainable Brands**

"Skip this book and you will steal from yourself. *The Five Thieves* offers a gift of awareness and a vision for finding peacefulness within ourselves and our society."
—**Noah Blumenthal, bestselling author of** *Be the Hero*

"*The Five Thieves of Happiness* is brilliantly conceived, beautifully written, and thoroughly engaging. John Izzo gently challenges, provokes, and nudges us to rethink our fundamental assumptions about the pursuit of happiness and how we may just be picking our own pockets of the well-being that we seek. It's a sparkling gem of a book, rich in timeless wisdom and abounding in contemporary truths—a book that you will want to return to again and again as you ponder what it means to live a good life."
—**Jim Kouzes, coauthor of** *The Leadership Challenge* **and Dean's Executive Fellow of Leadership, Leavey School of Business, Santa Clara University**

"I continue to be inspired by John Izzo as a professional and as a friend. I hope that *The Five Thieves of Happiness* can help you as much as he has helped me!"
—**Marshall Goldsmith, bestselling author of** *What Got You Here Won't Get You There*

"Happiness is a choice, but it requires effort and wisdom to pursue. In this thought-provoking book, Izzo helps identify the biggest stumbling blocks so that you can find a clearer path to sustained happiness and meaning in your life."

—**Shawn Achor, happiness researcher and** *New York Times* **bestselling author of** *Before Happiness*

"A powerful guide to becoming world-class happy."

—**Robin Sharma, #1 bestselling author of** *The Leader Who Had No Title* **and founder of The Titan Academy**

"Many people have spent many decades searching for the lost secret of happiness, but John Izzo is the one who found it and shows us how to steal it back, naturally! For anyone hoping to live better, this book is an essential—and perhaps life-changing—read."

—**Richard Leider, bestselling author or coauthor of** *The Power of Purpose*, *Repacking Your Bags*, *Life Reimagined*, **and** *Work Reimagined*

"Dr. John Izzo brilliantly depicts the five thieves that separate us from happiness. Not only does he powerfully explore what this means for each of us as individuals, but he elevates the conversation to the implications on society. This is a must-read for personal and societal transformation."

—**Arthur Woods, cofounder of Imperative**

"A new book by John Izzo is a cause for celebration. That's because Izzo tackles meaning and purpose in ways that are honest and hopeful. His latest book, *The Five Thieves of Happiness*, is no exception. In it, he challenges us to lean into our better nature and recapture a state that was ours to begin with: happiness. An important and entertaining read."

—**Mark Levy, author of** *Accidental Genius*

the
five thieves
of
happiness

Other books by John Izzo:

Stepping Up: How Taking Responsibility Changes Everything

Second Innocence: Rediscovering Joy and Wonder, a Guide to Renewal in Work, Relationships, and Daily Life

The Five Secrets You Must Discover before You Die

Awakening Corporate Soul: Four Paths to Unleash the Power of People at Work (Fairwinds Press, 1998)

the
five thieves
of
happiness

JOHN IZZO PhD

BK

Berrett–Koehler Publishers, Inc
a BK Life book

Berrett-Koehler Publishers, Inc.
1333 Broadway, Suite 1000, Oakland, CA 94612-1921
Tel: (510) 817-2277   Fax: (510) 817-2278   www.bkconnection.com

Ordering Information

Quantity sales. Special discounts are available on quantity purchases by corporations, associations, and others. For details, contact the "Special Sales Department" at the Berrett-Koehler address above.

Individual sales. Berrett-Koehler publications are available through most bookstores. They can also be ordered directly from Berrett-Koehler:

Tel: (800) 929-2929; Fax: (802) 864-7626; www.bkconnection.com.

Orders for college textbook/course adoption use. Please contact Berrett-Koehler:

Tel: (800) 929-2929; Fax: (802) 864-7626.

Orders by U.S. trade bookstores and wholesalers. Please contact Ingram Publisher Services, Tel: (800) 509-4887; Fax: (800) 838-1149; E-mail: customer.service@ingrampublisherservices.com; or visit www.ingrampublisherservices.com/Ordering for details about electronic ordering.

Berrett-Koehler and the BK logo are registered trademarks of Berrett-Koehler Publishers, Inc.

Printed in the United States of America

Berrett-Koehler books are printed on long-lasting acid-free paper. When it is available, we choose paper that has been manufactured by environmentally responsible processes. These may include using trees grown in sustainable forests, incorporating recycled paper, minimizing chlorine in bleaching, or recycling the energy produced at the paper mill.

Library of Congress Cataloging-in-Publication Data
Names: Izzo, John B. (John Baptist), 1957-- author.
Title: The five thieves of happiness / John Izzo, PhD.
Description: Oakland : Berrett-Koehler Publishers, [2017] | Includes bibliographical references and index.
Identifiers: LCCN 2016038083 | ISBN 9781626569324 (pbk.)
Subjects: LCSH: Happiness. | Conduct of life. | Spiritual life.
Classification: LCC BJ1481 .I99 2017 | DDC 158.1—dc23
LC record available at https://lccn.loc.gov/2016038083

21 20 19 18 17   10 9 8 7 6 5 4 3 2 1

Cover design by Nancy Austin. Interior design by Detta Penna. Composition by Gary Palmatier, Ideas to Images. Elizabeth von Radics, copyeditor; Mike Mollett, proofreader; Rachel Rice, indexer.

To Janice Halls,
my partner in life who teaches every day
what it means to claim happiness

contents

foreword

In nearly four decades as an executive coach, I have worked with some of the world's most influential leaders—brilliant, highly accomplished people who have made a positive difference in the lives of millions.

Recently, I coached three physicians who are standout exemplars: Dr. Jim Yong Kim, president of the World Bank; Dr. John Noseworthy, president of the Mayo Clinic; and Dr. Rajiv Shah, administrator of the United States Agency for International Development. As part of my coaching, I suggested they ask themselves a series of questions each day, one of which is *Did I do my best to be happy?*

It's a pretty simple question, and these men are smart, experienced, and highly credentialed. Yet they weren't sure what to say. "Do you have a problem with trying to be happy?" I asked.

In separate conversations, all three of them answered with virtually the same words: *It never occurred to me to try to be happy.*

Happiness can prove elusive, even for the best and brightest among us. If we are like these dedicated doctors and leaders, it isn't even on our radar. I suspect that a different kind of misapprehension is far more common—hoping for or expecting happiness but failing to attain it. In this thought-provoking book, John Izzo asks why happiness is so hard to grasp and why it matters to be happy. He makes a compelling case that we do better individually and collectively when we understand the "thieves" that try to rob us of our innate contentment.

As a philosophical Buddhist, I find that this concept makes perfect sense. Buddha named five hindrances that hold us back in meditation and in life: sensory desire, ill will, sloth, restlessness, and doubt. In our culture today, we are hindered to a great degree by John's thieves of happiness: control, conceit, coveting, consumption, and comfort.

The need for control is such a common issue among the leaders I coach and teach that I have developed an acronym to address it: *AIWATT*, which stands for, *Am I willing, at this time, to make the positive investment required to make a positive difference on this topic?* (If not, let it go.) Conceit, otherwise known as ego, is rampant in our fame-obsessed culture, and I have seen it do real damage in the lives of otherwise promising people. Coveting and consumption are nearly unavoidable in a consumer-driven economy as the great Western disease of *I will be happy when…* spreads around the globe. All of us, at one time or another, have been convinced that we'd be happy if only we could get that house, car, romantic partner, big promotion, or other object of our desire. Our need for comfort can lull us into the false perception that what we're doing is good enough, when in reality the world is demanding more of us.

If someone asked you to quickly name the five biggest thieves of your happiness, what would you say? It would be tempting to list your nasty boss, the spreadsheets you have to do, the bills you have to pay, or the terrible weather where you live. According to John's wise formulation, the thieves are all within us. That means we cannot blame anyone or anything outside ourselves if we aren't happy. It also means we have the power to connect with our inner happiness—though it takes great discipline to do it.

In my career and in my life, I place a high premium on happiness. I have been described in the press as a "happiness professional," a moniker I wholeheartedly accept. But it isn't always easy to maintain. I need help to keep up the practice. I suggest to my coaching clients that they ask themselves questions that reflect their most important priorities in life. I do this, too! Because I'm not always good at remembering the ritual, I have an assistant call me to read the questions to me over the phone, wherever in the world I happen to be. She always asks whether I did my best to be happy. I typically give myself a 9.3 or 9.4 out of 10. How do I achieve that?

Paradoxically, I don't. As John points out, happiness is not something to strive for. The only way to cure the disease is to choose happiness and meaning *now*—in the present moment. For example, in my book *Triggers* I write that we underestimate how much the environment affects us, and that is certainly true of me in an airport. For much of my career, I have been flying around the world to coach, speak, and teach. At first I was constantly beset by the aggravations of flying: planes leaving late, missing connections, being stuck in airports when I wanted to be anywhere else.

Then in 1984 I went to Africa with the American Red Cross African Famine Relief Campaign, a humanitarian mission on which I saw hundreds of people starve to death. It was an unforgettable experience that taught me something about being happy. Those people would have been overjoyed at the chance to be in an air-conditioned airport filled with places to eat and chairs to sit in. Before I came home, I made a commitment to myself: never complain because the airplane is late.

I fly every week. And every week I remember this commitment. Not long ago the computers were down in Chicago's O'Hare International Airport, and I couldn't get access to the lounge where I usually rest between flights. I started to get angry, but my long-ago commitment surfaced in my mind. *Be grateful. Be happy now. Don't wait.*

If you're stuck in an airport, or anywhere else you don't want to be, I hope you have a copy of this book with you. It will help you understand the inner forces arrayed against you.

Even better, it will guide you as you overcome those forces and connect to your deep, natural reserve of happiness.

Marshall Goldsmith
Author of *What Got You Here Won't Get You There: How Successful People Become Even More Successful* and *Triggers: Creating Behavior That Lasts— Becoming the Person You Want to Be*

preface

I have been a student of happiness and meaning my entire life. From my earliest memories, what has fascinated me most is trying to crack the code of what makes life worthy, meaningful, and happy. It was what led me into my professions (Presbyterian minister then author-speaker), to pursue my degrees (sociology, psychology, and religious studies), to write my books, and to engage in the research that has taken up my adult life. It has been a quest of the head and the heart. My mind wanted to know the secrets to happiness, and my heart wanted to live them.

Many of you may be familiar with my fourth book, *The Five Secrets You Must Discover before You Die*. The book was based on something I called the Wise Elder Project, in which I asked people to identify "the one older person they knew who had found true happiness and had something to teach us." After getting several thousand nominees, we interviewed 250 people between the ages of 60 and 102, with more than 18,000 years of life experience between them, who had only one thing in common: they were the happiest older person someone knew.

The Five Secrets helped me identify the secrets to lasting happiness, culled from the lives of this unique group. The response to the book was overwhelmingly positive. In letters and e-mails, people from all over the world told me that the five secrets made intuitive sense to them, but they also told me something else: knowing the secrets was not enough. In essence, they said, *I know what brings me happiness, but it's hard to put it into practice.*

Over the years since the book was published, it occurred to me that maybe the five secrets were only half the secret. When I interviewed those happy people, I was focused on what they *did* to find happiness, but later I started reflecting on what they had *not* done. It might be that there was something else that happy people did differently. Upon deeper reflection I realized that the people I had interviewed didn't seem particularly obsessed with finding happiness. In fact, their happiness seemed to be a by-product of how they saw the world, rather than the result of any particular quest or what was happening in their lives. A question rose up in me: *Did happiness really have to be that hard?*

In 2015 I decided to take an eight-month sabbatical from my work as an author, speaker, and consultant, in part because I felt I still had not fully cracked the code of sustainable happiness for myself. It was while on sabbatical, walking the Camino de Santiago in Spain, that the idea of the thieves of happiness first came to me. It was something like a gift from my subconscious, something I had somehow known for a very long time and yet consistently missed. It was like a clue to a puzzle that I had been trying to solve for a long while or a whodunit movie when some tiny clue finally clicks and you know who the culprit is. The eureka moment was this: maybe happiness is our natural state, but there are mental thought patterns that we let rob us of our happiness.

Over the course of the following 12 weeks, as I walked the Camino and later trekked in the Sacred Valley in Peru, I reflected on the question *Who are these thieves that rob our happiness?* One by one I began to name them. I claim no special inspiration for the five, but I believe I culled them from the various traditions that have studied happiness.

Having been a lifetime student of both the spiritual and philosophical traditions, as well as the discipline of psychology, I knew that the answer to this question was likely already there for the finding. Psychology and spirituality have one important shared quest. They both seek to answer the question *How do human beings find happiness and meaning?*

Throughout this book I draw from the spiritual traditions, as well as the scientific studies of psychology, to discover who these thieves are and how we can thwart them. All the thieves I discuss can be found in these traditions, though their names may vary. There could easily have been six or 10 thieves, but in the end I settled on the five that seemed to me the greatest robbers of our contentment.

As I reflected on the thieves, I contemplated how the same phenomenon was likely true for society. Just as I believe that our natural state as individuals is happiness, so I believe that the natural human state is of harmony and cooperation. Despite the common belief that this is a dog-eat-dog world, recent research into evolutionary biology suggests that human beings have thrived and become the dominant species on the planet precisely because of our cooperative nature. It is our capacity to cooperate across large numbers of strangers that allowed us to conquer the world, so to speak.

As I traveled the world for four decades, the vast majority of human beings I encountered, in many diverse cultures across six continents, seemed to be good and decent people. Why then was the evening news filled with unimaginable horrors, and why were we running like buffalo off a cliff toward environmental catastrophe when it seemed so obvious that change was needed?

Maybe the same thieves who were stealing our personal happiness were also robbing our societal harmony. After all, what was society but an outgrowth of each of our inner worlds writ large. This is why all global or community change must begin in the heart of each of us.

Some of the thieves will at first seem obvious to you, and they should be. The fact that you recognize their names tells you that we sense their presence already. But knowing who they are and kicking them out of your house are two very different things. It is my intention to show you who these thieves are, help you see how they steal our individual and societal happiness, and give you practical methods to get them out of your life.

chapter one

happiness is our natural state

A thief is someone who steals what is rightfully ours. This book is about the thieves we allow to rob us of the happiness that is our natural state. We don't need to seek happiness so much as we need to get out of its way. These same thieves rob us of the harmony we are capable of as a society.

Happiness is all the rage today. Books about happiness proliferate everywhere, it seems. The science of happiness has become big business, as well as the subject of scientific exploration. University studies seeking to discover, through clinical research, how happiness is engendered and maintained have become common at vaunted places like Harvard and the University of Michigan. I have written extensively about happiness, as well as lectured on it around the globe. In spite of all this attention, we live in a world awash in books and lectures on happiness, but unhappiness is all around us.

Is it possible that the very pursuit of happiness has within it the seeds of unhappiness? The idea of needing to seek happiness has, at its core, the belief that happiness and contentment are not our natural state, that somehow to find happiness we must go on a heroic quest to uncover that which will make us happy.

Even the label of being happy or unhappy can be a trap. By labeling ourselves as "unhappy," we are already sitting in judgment of our inner state. Some research has suggested that the act of assessing one's happiness on a consistent basis may actually lead to greater unhappiness, especially if we are feeling unhappy to begin with.[1]

happiness is not about happenings

The word *happiness* was chosen for this book with some trepidation. The word has many meanings to many different people. There are other words that could have been chosen, such as *contentment, peace, virtue, fulfillment, meaning, harmony,* and *joy.* Yet *happiness* appears to be the word of our time, the word that somehow in pop culture has come to symbolize our desire for a sense of rightness about life.

It is no accident that the English word *happiness* sounds an awful lot like *happenings.* The word *happiness* in most European languages, from Greek to English, originally was synonymous with the word *lucky* from the Middle English word *hap* (which meant "chance"). In other words, if you were fortunate enough to have good things happening to you, the result was the feeling of happiness.

In keeping with the origin of the word, most of us believe that happiness is directly related to happenings, even though we know it does not explain why some people appear to experience happiness regardless of what is happening in their lives, whereas others are chronically unhappy even with many good things happening around them.

The ancient Greeks had a slightly different notion of happiness. In many ways Aristotle began the conversation about happiness in the Western world when he identified it as the chief goal of a human life. The Greek word *eudaimonia* is more akin to the idea of human flourishing than the Middle English *happiness*. Though Aristotle granted that part of human flourishing came from external elements, such as health and wealth, he argued that happiness was more about living a life of virtue. He posited certain qualities of character that represented the more ideal state of a human, such as courage. The virtues were not so much moral qualities as they were ways of being that facilitate happiness. In other words, Aristotle introduced the idea that happiness was somehow related to an internal set of virtues or characteristics, which somehow filtered our experience.

Disconnecting happiness from happenings is critical to achieve lasting contentment. This is the happiness that each of us truly seeks—one that is not directly correlated with what is happening in our lives moment to moment but that has a robust lasting quality of its own regardless of outer circumstances.

happiness is our natural state

It is my contention that happiness is our natural state. But how do we define happiness? Happiness, contentment, a sense of well-being, the feeling that one's life has meaning and purpose—all are concepts most of us understand intuitively. We know it when we experience it, when there is a sense of things being well. When I use the word *happiness*, I mean it to be "a deep sense of rightness about one's life and a sense of inner contentment about oneself in the world." It is this very sense of the rightness of things that I argue is natural to us and is something that the thieves steal from us.

As was said on the first page of this book, one way to think about happiness is that we don't have to seek it so much as we need to get out of its way. We have been so trained to think that

we have to seek, long for, and work for happiness that it's easy
to forget that the contentment we seek is always there, waiting
for us to access it. Nature is a great teacher in this regard, which
is why so many of the wisdom and poetic traditions ask us to
approach nature as a role model. Research consistently shows
that when humans are surrounded by nature, especially trees
and other plants, we are happier and less stressed. There is a
reason for that. Nature appears to us to have the natural calm we
seek. Most of nature appears to simply *be*. It reminds us that we
also have that within us. Lao Tzu is purported to have said that
nature does not hurry, yet everything is accomplished.

The idea that the inner experience of happiness is our
natural state can be found throughout the spiritual traditions
of East and West. Whether or not you believe in the factual
truth of any or all of the great spiritual traditions, together they
represent humanity's collective quest for happiness over many
millennia. My intention here is not to support or promote any
particular religious viewpoint but to show that this notion that
we already have happiness is not new.

The Judeo-Christian-Islamic creation story illustrates this
through the story of Adam and Eve in the Garden of Eden.
Given the way humans have always seen nature as a teacher, it
is not surprising that one of the oldest stories in the West about
creation places the first humans happy and living in a garden.

The two first humans can do anything they want in the
garden except eat the fruit from the tree of the knowledge of
good and evil. Metaphorically, the tree represents the part of us
that judges and toils rather than experiences life. Before eating
from the tree, the first two humans simply enjoyed the garden.
They were, in essence, living in paradise, connected to their
natural happiness much like the trees and plants.

A snake entices them to eat from the tree, and immediately
they feel ashamed and realize they are naked. They cover up.

Rather than feel that they had all they needed, they suddenly felt they somehow needed something else to be happy. The divine creator finds them clothed and asks, "Who told you that you were naked?"

Rather than think of the physical act of being naked, the allegorical meaning is more like *Who told you that there was something you needed?* You are, after all, already in the Garden of Eden! Think about the image for a moment. In the West we use "the Garden of Eden" as a way of talking about a place where everything works. The initial thought of unhappiness, the sense that all is not just as it should be, does not come from any change in external circumstances but from a shift of internal perspective. The garden did not change, but the filter through which the garden is seen is what steals the natural sense of rightness.

The result of the act of eating the fruit of the tree is that humans are cursed to struggle from that point on. Sadly, many interpret this story as punishment when it is more about exile. Disconnected now from our true nature, which is to be happy, we lost the connection to our natural calm and, unlike the rest of nature, have been seeking happiness ever since.

In the Eastern tradition, yoga and meditation are used to quiet the mind to discover the inner calm that is already there. The original Sanskrit word for yoga means literally "to join" or "to unite." Unlike our modern idea of happiness, the word *yoga*, which is almost 5,000 years old, suggests not a seeking but a uniting with what is already within us. Many modern people think of yoga or even meditation as an arduous task to earn our way to calm rather than as a means to clear the mind so that one can rediscover the deep calm that is already our nature. Though suffering exists in the external world, the inner calm we seek is already within us. So when I say that happiness is naturally ours, that is what I mean.

A quote widely attributed to Rumi, a well-known thirteenth-century Persian poet, Islamic scholar, and Sufi mystic, says that the inspiration you seek is already within you. Be silent and listen. Again and again we see this idea that the experience of inner calm and happiness is already present.

We have glimpses of this inner calm not only in nature but in our own experiences, as well. The baby's natural smile is the most emblematic symbol of that inner state, the way the baby reaches out with curiosity to touch an object or explore the world without judgment.

The stillness of sleep in its most sublime moments is another image of the inner calm we already possess. Many in the Eastern tradition have compared the sense of oneness and calm we feel in sleep with our natural state of consciousness. Famous people like Shakespeare and D. H. Lawrence have extolled the virtues of sleep. As most occasional insomniacs know all too well, it is when we clear the mind and let sleep come, rather than seek it, that the peace of rest occurs. Happiness, like sleep, requires us to get out of its way. There is a reason we say, "sleeping like a baby"; somehow we know that the baby intuitively rests in the calm at the center of everything, a sleep soon disturbed by incessant seeking.

enter the thieves

But why use the metaphor of thieves to represent that which takes away our natural happiness and inner calm? A thief, by definition, is someone who takes away something that is already yours. In the case of happiness, the thieves are thought patterns and internal filters through which we see the world in a distorted way. They cloud our view of what is true and natural.

Most of the spiritual and wisdom traditions suggest the presence of distorted ways of seeing the world that must be avoided. In Buddhism there are the five hindrances: sensory desire, ill will, sloth, restlessness, and doubt. In the monastic tradition of Christianity, there are the seven deadly sins: pride, envy, gluttony, lust, anger, greed, and sloth. In Sikhism, the world's fifth-largest religion and one of its youngest, there is an idea that we as humans have a natural sense of the rightness of things, which Sikhs call *common sense*. Sikhism suggests that there are five thought patterns (which they actually call *thieves*) that rob us of the natural common sense we possess: lust, greed, attachment, rage, and conceit. All the traditions in essence teach us that we are naturally happy and in harmony, if only we tame these forces within us.

When I first mentioned this idea of the thieves of happiness to a friend, she immediately said, "So you mean the things we must avoid?" Yet this is not about having a list of things we must avoid, like items on a strict diet. A list of things we *must not do* could be as, or more, punishing than a list of things we *must do* to find happiness and contentment.

Rather it is useful, as I said, to think of the five thieves of happiness as thought patterns and internal filters through which we see the world.

As I reflected on the 250 happy older people I had interviewed for *The Five Secrets*, I realized that many of them had called out these thought patterns, though at the time I failed to grasp it. In essence, they told me that there are ways of thinking that will take you away from happiness. These thieves are not outside ourselves but rather filters that exist within us. To some extent the thieves are all very natural to us, but when these thought patterns "run the house" they radically change how we experience our lives.

the thieves are disguised as friends

Like any good thief, the five thieves often come with great disguises. A good thief looks like a friend before he robs us. As we explore each of the five thieves, you will see how the robber comes disguised as a constructive force in our lives but winds up tricking us. That is why the first path to getting the thieves out of the house is to recognize them for what they are.

The ultimate goal is to get these five thought patterns out of our lives, both individually and corporately. After all, if you have thieves in the house, you have to get rid of them. The five thieves are *control, conceit, coveting, consumption,* and *comfort.*

the thieves also steal societal happiness

Just as I argue that happiness is our natural state as individuals, the same can be argued for our species. There has been much debate over the centuries about the true nature of human beings. Are we inherently selfish or altruistic? Are we born to be miserable or to live in joy? Are we inherently loving or violent? Will we ultimately be a locust on planet Earth, taking away the earth's capacity to extend life? Or will we be like bees, bringing even more life to the earth than if we did not exist?

To answer the question of the true nature of the human species, it is worth pondering how *Homo sapiens* came to dominate the earth unlike any species in the history of life as we know it. Biologists such as Edward O. Wilson in his book *The Social Conquest of Earth* and Yuval Noah Harari in his book *Sapiens: A Brief History of Humankind* offer compelling evidence that what allowed human beings to thrive and conquer the earth is our unparalleled capacity to cooperate. Of course, humans competed with one another as well, and the history of war bears witness to this, but the real story of human progress is that of compassionate cooperation. Unlike any other species, we learned to cooperate with large numbers of strangers to accomplish common ends.[2]

In fact, there is evidence to suggest that much of our darker nature is a later development. For almost all of human history, perhaps 99 percent of our existence as a species, we lived in foraging tribes known as hunter-gatherers. This was who we were before the advent of agriculture. Although the evidence is scant, it turns out that our image of our ancient ancestors as warring savages is likely about as far from the truth as possible. Evidence suggests that our ancient ancestors displayed little violence toward other human beings, were likely quite compassionate, and cooperated extensively, including routinely sharing food. They also tended to see themselves as deeply connected to nature rather than at odds with it. Modern hunter-gatherer tribes continue to display this cooperative spirit. Evidence suggests that it was the agricultural revolution and the notion of property that helped foster what most of us associate with our darker human nature.[3]

This is not to suggest that humans are all good. But our truest nature—the most central feature of our collective self—is that of compassionate cooperator, and therein lies the root of our success. Much like our natural happiness, this true nature is obscured by shrouds of misconception.

The thieves are therefore as relevant to our community life as they are to our personal lives. It is my hope to show that the very things that rob us of our personal happiness also stand in the way of humanity's claiming our rightful place as a constructive, creative, and positive force on the planet. The community and the world are inherently a natural outgrowth of our inner life.

The house of humanity is nothing more than an extension of the inner houses of us as individuals. The inner state of each of us affects the state of the world. If we want a better world, each of us must work on the constructive nature of our own being. This is why all the spiritual traditions call upon us to work on our inner life before we try to save the world and why positive psychology suggests that prosocial behavior comes from inner happiness, not the other way around.

how i came to name the thieves

Before we launch into understanding and confronting the five thieves, you may want to know how I came to name them. Obviously, there could be countless thought patterns that might rob us of our natural contentment. As I walked the Camino and trekked in the Andes, the various thieves coalesced for me. Drawing less on science and more on both intuition and the wisdom traditions, I began to see the thought patterns that appeared through the various strands in my interviews for *The Five Secrets*, as well as my own life.

Drawing on the ancient traditions, each of the thieves bears resemblance to the thought patterns found in the five hindrances of Buddhism, the seven deadly sins of monastic Christianity, and the five thieves of Sikhism. The traditions name them differently, but at the core it seemed that control, conceit, coveting, consumption, and comfort were deeply relevant to our time and true to the wisdom of the traditions.

It is my hope that people of all beliefs, both secular and religious, will find in these strands of ancient wisdom the timeless truths of what stands between us and the calm contentment we so desire and the highest potential of human possibility.

chapter two

the first thief: control

Most of you probably know the story of the Buddha.
Siddhārtha Gautama is believed to have been born a
prince in India between 580 and 460 BCE.[1] His father wished
to protect him and prepare him for the life of a king, but he
had a premonition that if his son ever saw suffering he would
become a holy man. The king orchestrated the young prince's
life, prohibiting him from seeing religious gurus and surround-
ing him with youth so that he would not see the ravages of old
age, suffering, and death.

At the age of 29, Siddhārtha decided to leave the palace
grounds to meet his subjects. The story goes that soon after
leaving the palace, he encountered an old man, later a diseased
man, then a decaying corpse, and finally an ascetic (someone
who renounces the pleasures of earthly life to withdraw to a
simple lifestyle for spiritual reasons). Having never seen suffering or death, the prince realized that we age, that we get sick,
and that we ultimately die, and it sent him into a deep depression and ultimately into a period of years leading the life of an
ascetic, renouncing all earthly pleasures. Yet after his almost six

11

years of living the ascetic life, that path failed to alleviate his internal seeking.

After nearly dying at the age of 35, he found himself under a Bodhi tree, where he famously vowed not to rise until he had discovered a path out of the internal suffering in which all human beings are trapped. It is said that he sat there for 49 days until he found enlightenment and discovered what became known as the four noble truths.

Although it is not named as such, it is the thief we are about to explore that sent the Buddha on his journey. The first thief of happiness is named *control*. This thief wants us to believe that we can control life rather than accept life on its terms. The great truth that came to the Buddha was that what causes unhappiness is the craving for life to be other than what it is.

It is the nature of life that there are many things out of our control. As humans we will suffer, we will become sick, and we will ultimately die. These are the three truths about life that sent the young prince into a depression. He ultimately came to realize that it is not the hard truths about life that rob us of happiness, causing suffering, but rather our resistance to those truths. It is our craving for control that keeps us from true inner peace.

the monkey with the clenched fist

This thief makes us like the monkeys of Southeast Asia who were captured at one time by locals through a simple yet cruel trick. Sweets were placed all around a tree, and a coconut was hollowed out, leaving a hole just large enough for a monkey to slip his hand through. Inside was placed a sweet. The other side of the coconut had a bolt that was chained to a tree. When the monkeys came and ate the sweets spread around the tree, one monkey would inevitably pick up the coconut, reach inside, and grab the treat. But the hole was not big enough to get the clenched fist out.

The monkey would often try desperately to carry off the coconut, but, try as he might, the coconut could never be taken nor the sweet removed from its shell. The only thing the monkey had to do to be free was unclench his fist and let go of the sweet. Yet most monkeys fought until utterly exhausted. The islanders would simply capture the monkey in that exhausted state. The monkey's undoing was his own attachment and inability to let go.

attention without attachment

Happiness is knowing what we can control and accepting what we cannot control. At the most basic level, happiness comes from understanding that we *can* control our actions and our responses to things external to us, but we *cannot* control the results of our actions. Focusing on our actions brings happiness; focusing on the result of our actions brings unhappiness.

The Buddha and Jesus often appear to the casual reader to be very different in their approaches to enlightenment or salvation (the two terms used in each tradition). In fact, the more one examines the teachings of each, the more one sees the way that both teachers emphasize the need to surrender to that which is at any moment. This is why the Buddhist Thích Nhất Hạnh has written extensively about the similarities of each teacher.

When Jesus encouraged his followers to look to the flowers of the field as role models because they did not seek, he was making a very important spiritual point. When he said, "Who of you by worrying can add a single hour to your life?"[2] he was making the same point. It is not the lack of control that brings suffering but the desire for control, which keeps us from lasting happiness and peace.

One of the big moments in my own life was when I first understood the distinction between attention and attachment. *Attention* is the energy and choices I make, whereas *attachment* is an inner desire to control what is inherently uncontrollable. Another way to think about this is to see it as intention without tension. Having goals in life, or even desires of what we want to happen in any particular situation, is not a problem in terms of our happiness. It is when we become attached to controlling an outcome that the thief starts to rob us. The theft of our happiness rarely comes from our intentions but from the tension we feel when attached to the outcomes of things.

How do we know the difference between attention and attachment? Attention is about taking action in the present moment toward hoped-for ends, whereas attachment is becoming wedded to a particular outcome's being the source of our happiness.

I play a great deal of tennis, and this point can be illustrated easily there. Happiness on the tennis court is found in the experience of the body playing the game, the joy of experiencing the way the body, the racquet, and the ball all become one. In my most sublime moments playing tennis, my focus is simply on being fully present in the game, attentive to how I am hitting the ball and moving my feet. The moment I become focused primarily on whether I am going to win a point is the very moment when tennis becomes a source of unhappiness. Of course, I have the intention of winning a point and even the match, but this is an outcome I cannot control. What I can control is my intention to be as fully in the game as possible at every moment.

Life is much like that tennis game. We are happiest when we are simply fully present in each moment, expressing our intention through our focus and unattached to the outcome as the source of happiness.

Often we discover that the outcome—the goal we have become attached to—turns out to be less rewarding than the striving (the intention). My partner, Janice, tried out for the national baseball team in Canada for 18 years! For almost two decades, she worked hard, played hard, and practiced hard, and every year she tried to win a spot on the roster. Every year she failed to make it until finally, after all those years, she was given a spot. You would think, of course, that the outcome would have been the highlight of all that struggle. The opposite turned out to be the case. Getting on the team was anticlimactic compared with the present-moment focus, year after year, of trying to be the best player she could possibly be, both on the field and in the inner mental game. Besides, she could not control the outcome, so the more she focused on the process, the happier she was.

control is an illusion; the present moment is real

Two of the most obvious things we try to control are the past and the future. Of course, we cannot control that which has already happened, and we cannot control that which has not yet occurred. The twins of regret and worry (first cousins of control) take away moment-to-moment contentment. Each time we find ourselves indulging in regret or worry, we are letting this thief take away our natural state of being present.

One of the things the thieves do is rob us of something that is naturally ours and leave in its place a false truth that brings us misery. This thief puts on the disguise of intentionality, which is a good thing, then robs us of our happiness by making us focus on controlling the outcomes of our life. Being in the present moment, accepting whatever is at that moment (letting go of the clenched fist) is the door to happiness, but the thief wants us to believe that if we try hard enough we will be able to control the outcomes of our life.

all suffering is resistance to whatever is

A principle to bear in mind is that almost all internal suffering comes from resistance to whatever is true at any moment. It is not the happenings of our life that lead to unhappiness but the desire to control them rather than accept whatever the present moment serves up. Don't confuse this acceptance with passivity. Remember intention without tension, focus without attachment. Wanting or trying to achieve something is not the source of unhappiness, but the desire for control of outcome is.

Imagine, for example, a person who grew up believing that one day they would win a gold medal in the Olympics. There is nothing wrong with wanting a gold medal, but if I crave a gold medal as the source of my happiness, the love of the sport itself will elude me. Every experience will merely be either a step toward or away from that goal. If I don't achieve the goal, disappointment will be my reward. The word for "attachment" in Tibetan is *dö chag,* which literally means "sticky desire." Desire is good; a sticky attachment to outcome is not. That person cannot control getting a gold medal, but they can be fully present in all the steps toward that goal. This also means not being resistant to whatever natural element you find yourself in; seek only to ask how you can flourish in that element.

Nature is a great teacher about the practice of nonresistance in this way. When I was on my self-imposed sabbatical in the Peruvian Andes, I thought of this when I saw a small tree that had literally grown atop a boulder in a river. The tree would surely have preferred to have taken seed in a nice clearing in the woods, where life would be easy, but this is the place it found itself. In this unlikely place, it had flourished by working with the elements around it rather than resisting them.

Although a present-moment focus—being always in the present moment—is most strongly associated with Buddhism, the value of focusing on the present appears in nearly all spiritual and philosophical traditions. Many people mistakenly believe that the secret to happiness is to have this present-moment focus, but the real secret is to let go of control. We tell ourselves to "stay in the moment," as if just by staying in the moment we will be happy. What we miss is that staying in the moment is not what brings happiness. What brings inner peace is acceptance of whatever is happening in the present moment. There is nothing inherently unhelpful about thinking about the future or about the past; it is the desire for control that changes the landscape.

Let me illustrate. If I sit for an hour and daydream about the future, let's say a trip I am to take soon or my coming wedding day, this can be a very pleasurable activity. Likewise I could spend an hour reminiscing about a pleasant or even painful past experience of my life. This too can be pleasurable and perhaps even useful, if it gives me insight into my current choices.

The problem arrives when control shows up. As we think about our wedding day, we may fret that it might rain, or what if Uncle Bill drinks too much and gets angry, or maybe I won't be as beautiful a bride as my sister was, and on it goes. The thief knows we have no control over these things but keeps telling us that if we worry enough (hold our fist tight enough), somehow we will find peace. The opposite of course is true: when we imagine future things that may happen that worry us, we must be mindful of the thief and brush it aside. The future cannot be controlled, only experienced. Happiness does not depend on that outcome.

There is also nothing inherently unhelpful about reflecting on the past. For example, I might find myself thinking about a failed relationship, along with mistakes I might wish to correct. The feelings of regret are not the source of unhappiness so much as the desire to control the past. Of course, I have no control over that. The past is what it is. We can learn from it and carry new intentions into our present decisions. So long as I mindfully accept that which is at any given moment, including the past, I am always keeping the thief in its proper place. Many people spend hours of misery wishing they could relive decisions from their past when what is required is simple acceptance.

Don't confuse letting go of control with becoming passive about influencing the course of your life. Remember that it is not the intention that brings unhappiness; it is the attachment.

training your mind to let go of control

Being forced into an experience that keeps you firmly in the present moment, surrendering that false sense of control that may give you tentative relief but never true inner peace, can be a very powerful thing. The thief robs us of our natural capacity to be in the present, accepting whatever is at each moment (attention without tension) and leaves in its place the false belief that if I try hard enough to control all that surrounds me, I will find peace.

One of the experiences that taught me to keep this thief at bay was walking the Camino de Santiago in northern Spain in the summer of 2015. The Camino is a 750-kilometer pilgrimage that Christians have been taking for a thousand years, ending at the Cathedral of Santiago de Compostela in Galicia, Spain, where the bones of the Apostle James are believed to be buried. Although it was once a spiritual experience exclusively for Christians, *The Way,* as it is often referred to, is now walked by people of all faiths, ages, and persuasions for many reasons.

My reasons for walking the Camino were several, among them to learn to be more fully present moment to moment. I walked an average of about 20 miles per day. The day would often start with two hours of walking, at or just before sunrise, to arrive for a light breakfast at the first place that seemed right that morning. As I began the day, I never knew how far I would walk, where I would stay, whom I might meet, or how my body would react.

In the beginning of my journey, I tried to map out each day, control with whom I would walk, determine where and what I would eat, plan the village where I would sleep, and so on. Yet it was not long before I realized that the Camino had its own lessons to teach. All the things I wanted badly to control became so evidently out of my control as the miles and days passed.

Some days my body was in the mood to walk forever, and other days some small muscle pull, a problem with a foot, the heat of the day, or an encounter with a fellow pilgrim (the word given to those who walk the Camino, *peregrine* in Spanish) would dictate the pace. I often had my mind set on staying in a particular village or hostel, only to discover that all the beds were already taken. My mind would get set on that wonderful freshly squeezed Valencia orange juice and the homemade potato tortillas from the cafés consumed gleefully for several days, only to discover that for the next five days the search for what had been omnipresent was in vain. It was not long before I began to see the parallel between the walk on the Camino and the walk of life. The more I took the Camino as it came to me, rather than being wedded to some perfect plan, the greater the contentment and peace I discovered.

Yet it was my desire to control other people that taught me the most powerful lessons on the Camino. On the first few days of my journey, I met two German pilgrims whom I liked a great deal. Walking with them was enjoyable, and we struck up an immediate friendship. For the first few nights, we stayed in the same hostels, often in multibed rooms. Then one morning as we began our day, one of them said, "I am going to stay longer for breakfast." The other companion started to walk faster than I, and soon she too was gone. I had become wedded to walking with them for many days, but suddenly both of them were gone and I was on my own.

I so much wanted to control my Camino experience. As the walk continued, some of the people I connected with would show up again and again. Others shared with me an amazing hour of deep spiritual connection, never to appear again. The thief kept me wanting to control whom I connected with and how long we stayed connected, to avoid the loss of people I had come to care about or even to conjure up just the right person when needed.

It was not my intentions that caused me to suffer but my attachment to control. Because intent isn't wrong, I realized that my desire to connect with certain people wasn't the problem. But I couldn't control the desires of others or the various circumstances that might cause my path to diverge from theirs. After more days and miles went by, more and more I found myself staying in the present moment, open to all that might appear. When the thief would show up, I gently noticed it and ushered it to the door.

Think of all the things in your life that you want to be constant. Think of the expectations we hold on to about our careers, the goals we must achieve, the people in our lives, and even the events of a particular day. Know that having intentions is fine but that holding on to them like that monkey, when life is not under your control, will bring you unhappiness. The more you allow this metaphor to sink into your conscious mind, the more you will see how we cling to control, how we bang the coconut of life against a tree, trying to set the sweet free. But freedom is found not inside the coconut but in the unclenching of the fist in the present moment, accepting whatever is happening right now.

control in relationships

The thief shows up in our daily relationships as well. For example, we spend much of our time trying to control others, leading to unending internal suffering. If you are angry at me and I apologize, I want very much to control your reaction. My desire for your forgiveness robs me of my happiness, when I should focus on what I can control, which is my sincere apology. This is a subtle but important distinction. Focusing on my apology is within my control; how you respond to it is not.

Perhaps I want to control how my intimate partner feels loved. Perhaps for me love is expressed through touch, but for my partner love is experienced through acts of service or kindness. My desire to control the other's experience of love will cause me a great deal of suffering, whereas an acceptance of how they experience love will bring me peace. It seems to me that the source of much suffering in intimate relationships comes from the presence of control, when we want our partners to act and be the way *we* want them to be.

Let me share a personal example. My ex-wife and I were together for 15 years. Although there were many downs in the relationship, there were also moments of incredible happiness, joyous experiences with our family, as well as good work that we did together. After we split, my ex seemed to feel the need to diminish our relationship and to see the time we spent together as a "mistake" and perhaps a waste of those precious years. She rarely talked about the good times, focusing instead on the ways we had disappointed each other. For me those years had been a time of great learning for both of us and a necessary part of our journey. Together we had done important work in the world and likely discovered important aspects of ourselves while bringing inspiration to others.

For several years after we ended the relationship, I had a strong desire to get her to see those years the way I did, to have her validate to me that she saw them as worthy. She would often show up in my dreams, which always involved, in some form, my trying to resolve this difference. Then one day a good friend said to me, "You want to control how she sees your years together and expresses that to you, but you cannot do it. You can control only how *you* see your years together."

In that moment it was as if a veil was suddenly lifted from my eyes. The thief of my happiness was my desire to control that which I was unable to control. It was not her view of our life together that took away my peace; it was my unrealistic focus on controlling her view. From that moment forward, whenever I had the desire to seek that validation from her I would instead focus on what I could fully control, which was my seeing those years as precious and important even if tumultuous. I let go of my sticky desire for an outcome over which I had no control. Interestingly, to this day she has never again visited me in dreams as an unresolved conflict.

surrender—the oppositional force

The opposite of control is *surrender:* complete acceptance of whatever is at any moment. Here is a simple example. All day long you are looking forward to a game of golf, but the weather forecast is dicey. There is a 50 percent chance of rain. You anxiously watch the skies and check the weather radar and forecast. You know, of course, that you cannot control the weather, but you persist. You cling to the idea of needing to play that game to be happy. When your tee time approaches, the sky is clear, only to suddenly darken, leading to a washout. The thief has ruined your entire day. Rather than surrender to that which is—it may rain or it may not, and I have no control over either outcome—you resist what simply is. Surrender literally means to stop fighting the natural flow of things.

It is not about inaction; it's about taking action from a place of what I call *surrender energy*. There is no problem with reflecting on what my plan B will be if the game is rained out or on how I might fit the game in next week. What I won't do is let control keep me from the simple act of surrendering to whatever is happening right now.

This thief is also very tricky, affecting us in very subtle ways. A friend of mine is in a relationship in which there was a betrayal by her male partner. The couple almost split up over it. She told me recently that she used to long for him to ask her to marry him and that she would proudly wear his ring. Now she says she no longer desires that ring because "what if one day he decides to leave me again, and I am left with the embarrassment of his choosing to leave me as his wife rather than his girlfriend?"

Our desire to control often means we want to control future hurt, emotions, and events that may or may not occur. In this case, my friend and her partner had made great progress as a couple since the betrayal. They were well on their way to building a better relationship than they had ever had. Yet she wanted to control the possibility of embarrassment and hurt that might happen down the road. By allowing the thief to trick her into thinking that she could control all future hurt, she was actually fencing out the possibility of truly having what she wanted, which was a long-term commitment. Of course, she might get hurt and her partner could embarrass her again, but by allowing the thief to dominate, she was fencing out true happiness as much as potential hurt.

This thief wants us to wall ourselves off in some safe corner with a helmet on so that we can protect against every eventuality. But as the Buddha discovered when he left the palace, we cannot control the possibility of suffering, but we *can* choose to tame our desire for control, ultimately leading to inner contentment. When the thief is banned, we can take life on its own terms and then sit like the Buddha, calm and ready for that which is.

kicking the thief out of your house

At this point you hopefully see how the thief named control robs us of our happiness. But how do we get the thief out of the house? The first step is to recognize that this is *your* house. Many spiritual traditions speak of the mind as a temple or a palace. This is a helpful metaphor because a temple is a sacred place, meant to be cared for in the most meticulous manner. Your inner house is the temple of your happiness. Because your happiness resides in the temple of your mind, it is your prerogative to decide who gets into that temple and who gets to stay.

Although perhaps apocryphal, there is an instructive story about someone the Buddha encountered soon after his experience under the Bodhi tree. A stranger he passed on the road was so struck by the Buddha's calm radiance that he asked him, "Are you a god?"

The Buddha replied, "No. I am not."

"What are you then?" the man asked.

And the Buddha simply said, "I am awake."

The peace that the Buddha exuded was simply that of one who was awake.

Being awake is about being mindful—truly noticing what is going on. A simple definition of *mindfulness* is "the practice of maintaining a nonjudgmental state of heightened or complete awareness of one's thoughts, emotions, or experiences on a moment-to-moment basis."[3] To be awake and mindful is to have a heightened sense of awareness of what is going on in your inner mind, the temple of your happiness.

The two key elements of mindfulness are moment-to-moment awareness and nonjudgment. When we are mindful, we are consistently aware of what is happening in our inner mind and in a place of curiosity rather than judgment. Once we understand these two concepts, we are prepared to learn how to master the thieves. Though we want to kick them out of the house, we must recognize that a thief is part of our own inner nature, not some foreign visitor. Humans like to control things, and at times that serves us well; but when we let our desire for control rule the house, we find misery rather than happiness.

We cannot always control our instinctual thoughts, but we can be mindful by noticing them, by being in a place of non-judgment, and then choosing a different path. We can decide what thought patterns get a permanent bedroom in our inner temple. We must recognize that the thoughts we allow to rule us are a choice. But many people act as though they are not in charge of their own minds, such as wanting to control the future by incessant worrying.

The final and most critical aspect of mindfulness is the capacity to gently brush aside something once we become aware of it. This step is critical when it comes to changing any behavior that ultimately doesn't serve us.

To explain this let me tell you about my first experiences learning meditation. My first meditation teacher was Deborah Klein, who was the wife of my co-author for my first book, *Awakening Corporate Soul: Four Paths to Unleash the Power of People at Work*. Deborah had practiced yoga for many years. Although the core idea of meditation is to quiet the mind, training it to stay in the present moment, the greater goal of meditation is to become the master of the inner temple. Many people talk about what is called the *monkey mind,* which is a Buddhist term meaning "unsettled; restless; capricious; whimsical; fanciful; inconstant; confused; indecisive; uncontrollable."[4] The goal of meditation is to train the mind to be the opposite of this: aware, awake, and constant.

When I first started meditating, it was difficult to quiet my mind; some worry, task, or thought would invade my peace. I asked Deborah, "What do I do when distracting thoughts come into my mind?"

She said, "When a distracting thought comes into your mind, I want you to simply be aware of it and then imagine your hand gently brushing it aside, as if to say, 'Not now.'"

In other words, with no judgment or resistance but instead with calm awareness, notice the thought and then sweep it aside. This is a subtle but important part of working with thieves and training our minds for happiness. The last thing we should do is scold ourselves for the thief's presence. That which we resist persists.

I admit that it took many hours of training before this distracted mind could be trained to focus. In the beginning it felt like I was having to constantly imagine my hands brushing aside thoughts. But soon I realized a powerful truth, one that forever changed how I saw everything in my inner world. I realized that I am awake and alert; I am in control of my mind. The temple has a ruler, and it is me. Soon the habit of clearing the mind dominated the habit of allowing whatever thought arrived to take up residence.

the three steps

Let's apply this idea of mindfulness to the thieves. When I am going through my day and a thief arrives, I follow three simple steps: *notice, stop,* and *replace.* First we recognize the presence of the thief, then we stop the thief by gently brushing it aside, and then we choose to allow a different thought to dominate. To build on the thief metaphor, we must first catch the thief (notice), then arrest the thief (stop), and then throw the thief out or at least reform it (replace).

Here is an illustration from an earlier example. I have my heart set on playing golf this evening because I believe that golf will make me happy on this day. I obsessively keep checking the iffy forecast all morning and afternoon. My day's contentment is being dampened by my desire to control the weather. Remember that almost all suffering comes from resistance to whatever is at any moment. The thing itself is not what causes the suffering; it is the *resistance* to that which is happening at any moment that is the source of suffering. I notice that the thief is present—the desire to control the future rather than surrender to whatever is. I notice the thief, and then I choose to gently show him the door and accept that I cannot change the weather.

But there is an important third step. The thief has been noticed and its disguise removed. I have stopped the inner dialogue that robs me of my happiness (*To be happy I must be in control*), but now I must take the third critical step, which is to replace.

To replace means to have ready at hand a new thought pattern or filter through which to see my life. In this case, that alternative view is to accept whatever is at any moment and to embrace what might emerge; that is, I see that I cannot control the future or the outcome of a situation, so I show the thief the door, sending it out of my house and in its place bringing in a new belief system that is open to whatever is at any moment, knowing that only my intentions are within my control.

The same could apply to my friend who was betrayed. First she must notice that the thief is holding her back from recommitting to her relationship fully. She knows that she might get hurt but recognizes that she can control only her present-moment intentions. She notices the thief and arrests it. But then she must replace the filter of control with an acceptance of whatever is at this very moment and a willingness to take life as it emerges. Happiness and calm replace worry.

Of course, you are right in thinking, *It is not that easy.* The untrained mind is like that monkey mind. It is like when I first tried to meditate and was frustrated because I could not quiet my mind. Now, years later, meditation is natural for me, and most of the time I can easily quiet my mind. So it is with the thieves: at first when you notice, stop, and replace, you will find it difficult. Your mind will tell you that it is simply impossible. But not only is it possible, but unless you arrest the thief and throw it out, you will never find lasting happiness.

I suggest trying what I call the *two-week effort.* For the next two weeks, practice becoming aware of every moment in which either you believe a particular outcome is required for you to be happy or you find yourself resisting whatever is at any moment. Then practice the three steps: notice the thief, stop the thief, and replace the thief with the words *I choose to be fully present, embracing what is at this very moment.*

You might, for example, find yourself in a traffic jam at the end of a tiring day at work. You long for the relaxation of your sofa and the company of your partner but find yourself stuck in your car with no idea how long it will take to get home. In that moment notice how your desire to control and your attachment to being at home is robbing you of your happiness. Arrest the thief by gently showing it the door, as if to say, "You are not going to rob me." Then replace the thief with a new thought pattern: *I choose to be fully present, embracing what is right now. My happiness is here, not there in the outcome of being home.* You may just find that your focus now shifts toward how to make this moment stuck in traffic as happy as it can be. Like the tree that took seed on a boulder, you will seek ways to flourish, even in the traffic jam.

When it comes to replacing thought patterns, one of the most helpful aids are mantras. A *mantra* is a sound, word, or phrase repeated continually by someone who is praying or meditating. Although *mantra* is a Sanskrit word that literally means "instrument of thought" (or a tool for thinking), short phrases and sounds are found in almost all Eastern and Western traditions. Mantras are a great way to train your mind for happiness. Though mantras were originally mostly sounds in the early Vedic tradition, today mantras can take the form of a phrase or a set of words repeated frequently to alter your state of mind.

A mantra for banishing control can be found in these simple words:

> *I choose to be in the present moment and to embrace whatever is. Happiness is not in the outcome I seek.*

control in society

As mentioned earlier, the world as we know it, what we often call "society," is an extension of the inner house of our individual lives. Control affects our community life in profound ways.

A good example of this is our desire to control others by getting them to see the world as we do. We often get angry when someone we love, or even a stranger, holds a view that is different from ours. Each of us is wedded to our own way of seeing the world, often with the effect that we are not open to learning from the views of others. Much of the political rancor in the United States, for example, is driven by the desire to control our own emotions when others disagree with us. Psychologists call this *cognitive dissonance*.

Most human beings want an internal world with few con-tradictions. In 1957 the social psychologist Leon Festinger first proposed cognitive dissonance theory, which states that people have a powerful motive to maintain cognitive consistency. We want to hold our beliefs and feel as little internal conflict about those beliefs as possible, but this desire to control internal con-flict keeps us from having authentic dialogue with those who disagree with us.

When our beliefs are challenged, a discrepancy is evoked, resulting in a state of tension known as *dissonance*. Because the experience of dissonance is unpleasant for most people, we are motivated to reduce or eliminate it and achieve *consonance*, or internal agreement between our beliefs and the outside reality. We seek to alleviate the pain we feel from being out of control by finding information and people who will validate our way of seeing the world.

The connected world of the Internet is a perfect milieu for us to avoid dissonance and for control to dominate our relationships with one another. Although the Internet allows us to explore many views that are divergent from our own, it also allows us to expose ourselves to the views of only those with whom we agree. By so doing we reduce any dissonance we might feel that our attitudes and beliefs might not be the full truth and widely shared. We want to control our internal con-flict even though we might learn something by allowing our-selves to experience that conflict. We resist the possibility that our views might be shaped and that as a society we might learn from one another and thus find greater common ground. By letting go of the illusion that the whole world can be controlled by my point of view, I can suddenly entertain the possibility of learning from others.

Let me make this real. The United States is locked in a nearly two-decade divide between right and left. People are afraid to talk about politics with anyone other than those who they know already agree with them. Many friends have told me about heated arguments that occur within families and even at work. Rarely is there any productive dialogue between the right and the left. There is little doubt that this is bad for the country and for creating a civil society that manages to solve complex problems.

One reason for this lack of dialogue, though not the only one, is that everyone is trying to protect themselves from dissonance. We hold on to our viewpoints even though that attachment ultimately constrains all Americans in an uncivil society. This often means we seek news that primarily supports our current mental models. During the presidential election of 2012, for example, it is not surprising that the most-watched network during the Republican convention was Fox, whereas during the Democratic Convention it was MSNBC and CNN.[5] Because it is quite likely that more Republicans watched their own convention and more Democrats watched theirs, that means most people watched the television station that would most confirm their existing views rather than challenge them, a phenomenon known as *confirmation bias.*

The irony is that both conservatives and liberals are trying so hard to control and hold on to their beliefs about the world and about each other that they want to listen mostly to people who already agree with them. By doing so they control the dissonance or suffering they might feel (and the anger that might well up in them) when they listen to views different from their own. We stay in control. But the problem is that if each of us seeks only to validate our own views, there will be no learning and no possibility of finding middle ground. We rarely learn much by talking to those whose views mirror our own.

The next time you have a conversation with someone who disagrees with you, or see something that contradicts your confirmation bias, be aware of the thief. It tries to keep you from feeling any dissonance about reconsidering your beliefs. Instead of reacting by clinging to your beliefs or withdrawing, be mindful.

Having spent time in both Israel and the Palestinian territories in the Middle East, I saw this phenomenon firsthand. It can also be seen between free-market capitalists and those who want to rein in the markets, and between those who are pro-business and those who are pro-environment. By encouraging us to keep dissonance at bay, the thief robs us of opportunities for true dialogue. And we need dialogue to have a civil society.

Some will say that it is not control that prevents us from considering other viewpoints or seeking information that challenges our deeply held beliefs but rather a firm moral conviction that we are correct. My point is not that we should forgo strong convictions, nor am I suggesting that some beliefs don't have more objective validity than others. Rather we need to recognize that when we try to control others by needing them to agree with us and when we try to avoid any discomfort we feel about our beliefs being challenged, we create a community in which harmony becomes increasingly difficult. Our attachment to our ideas and beliefs can be as destructive to the social good as our attachment to controlling events and people is to our personal happiness.

the story of jack

As a young theology student in Chicago in 1980, I had an experience that showed me how damaging control can be.

One of my classes was taught by a professor who held very liberal views. Dr. Collins thought that the Bible was not to be taken literally; instead she encouraged us to think critically about how the scriptures came to be written. She suggested that many of the events found in the Gospels, which chronicle the life of Jesus, likely did not happen the way they were reported and that some of words spoken by Jesus might have been attributed to him by others at a later date.

I struggled in Dr. Collins's class. It was tough to have some of my core beliefs challenged. The thief wanted me to stop listening. But hard as it was, it seemed important for me to entertain her ideas and consider them fully. But Jack, one my classmates, was having a much more difficult time. He often had heated arguments with Dr. Collins during class. As the semester went on, he became angrier.

Finally, I asked him, "Jack, why do you let her get to you this way? It is only one class, and she's only one professor."

He thought for a moment and then said, "John, I could let it go, but what if she is right?"

At that moment I fully understood what was really going on. Jack didn't want to be challenged by new ideas. He wanted to control his belief system, hold on to the sweet in the coconut, even though he felt it now chained him. His attachment to those beliefs as the source of his happiness was making him suffer.

In the end I agreed with some of Dr. Collins's conclusions and disagreed with others. But by allowing myself to realize that I could learn even in the presence of dissonance, I furthered my education and deepened my faith. Staying present became a source of strength. I remained in seminary and went on to become an ordained Presbyterian minister. Jack dropped out and, as far as I know, gave up his pursuit of the ministry.

letting go of the clenched fist

This thief robs personal happiness and societal harmony. If we let it rule our lives, we are indeed like those monkeys, hand clenched inside a trap from which we cannot escape until we finally let go. Control is an illusion; surrendering to and accept-ing whatever is at any moment is the path to contentment: attention without tension, living in the present moment with-out attachment.

As I was walking the Camino, I approached León, a city I had dreamed of for days. Somehow it felt like arriving there would bring some greater happiness; but by the time I could see the city, I was finally letting go of everything but the present moment and had penned this poem:

> You'd dreamed of Leon for days
> But now that you could see it
> Could hardly Remember why it had mattered to get
>   there at all
> All the Leons of our life Are a distraction from Now
> The present, Open to everything that might reveal itself
> Once you were a man who dreamed always,
> of far off destinations where Happiness would surely
>   reside
> But slowly, gently, Came to see There is no there
> Only here, only Now
> In the one place where happiness always arrives

four ways to banish the first thief

- In each moment surrender to whatever is happening. Control and influence what you can while choosing to accept whatever is at that moment.

- Accept the hard truths about life. Death, suffering, pain, loneliness, and sorrow are as much a part of the human experience as are joy, living, companionship, and happi-ness. Remember that it is the craving for things to be dif-ferent, not the circumstance, that robs you of happiness.

- Know that you cannot control the past or the future. When you feel pain about the past or worry about the future, accept that only the present moment is real and gently choose to come back into that moment.

- Practice the three steps for two weeks: notice, stop, and replace. Become aware of control and begin to train your mind to kick that thief out of your house. This takes practice, but once it is mastered your natural contentment will blossom.

mantra

I choose to be in the present moment and to embrace whatever is. Happiness is not in the outcome I seek.

chapter three

the second thief: conceit

This next thief is one the most powerful robbers of happiness. It is perhaps the single greatest barrier to true contentment and even societal well-being. The second thief of happiness is *conceit*—an overemphasis on your personal importance, a belief that you are separate from others and that only by distinguishing yourself can you find happiness. Another word for this thief is *ego*.

At the heart of conceit is the idea of separation. When we see ourselves as separate from others, from the community and perhaps from life itself, we become so focused on our own small self that we lose sight of our true nature. One of the great findings of modern quantum physics is the way that matter and energy are connected. Atoms separated by time and space influence other atoms in spite of no physical connection. Separation as we know it may actually be an illusion.

This thief causes us to constantly obsess about our place in the world. It keeps us asking questions like *What is my status? What is my rank? How will I find happiness? What will happen to me when I die? Why am I here? Where do I fit? Am I important?*

Feel the weight of these questions! The *I* and the *me* are at the heart of conceit, and whenever our world revolves around the ego, we are bound to lose the happiness that is rightfully ours.

Imagine for a moment if you defined your happiness as connecting to the whole rather than differentiating from the whole. What if you did not have to find your place to be happy? What if you were already part of a whole that had meaning? What if the very focus on your own happiness and your ego was the very thing robbing you of happiness? That is, could it be that the very thing you think is the source of your happiness is the cause of your misery?

the myth of narcissus

In this way the second thief is like Narcissus, one of the most well-known figures from Greek mythology. Narcissus was a hunter known for his beauty. He was so focused on himself that he rejected and scorned all suitors. One of those suitors fell on his sword at Narcissus's doorstep and, before he died, prayed to the gods that Narcissus might be taught a lesson for all the pain he caused others.

That lesson came as Narcissus walked by a pool and stopped to drink, only to see his own beautiful image in the water. So entranced was he by his own reflection that he fell in love with it. Though there are numerous versions of the myth, several hold that he remained by the pool, trying in vain to capture the object of his desire. Each time he would reach into the water to capture the image, it would disappear. Eventually, he became so filled with sorrow that he took his own life.

Although the myth of Narcissus can be seen merely as a story about physical beauty, there is a deeper, more profound lesson. The ego—and a focus on the self as the source of one's happiness—is much like the beauty the handsome Greek sought in his reflection. It is important to note that he took his own life because he ultimately couldn't possess the image of his own ego. That for which he sought—which is what we all seek—can be found only when we take our eyes off the ego and look up. As one of the wise elders I interviewed for *The Five Secrets* told me, "The ironic thing about happiness is that when you are seeking it for yourself, it eludes you; but when you look up and serve something bigger than yourself, happiness finds you."

Intuitively, we all know this to be true because the moments we have been happiest are rarely the moments when we were most focused on ourselves but rather when we got lost in something outside ourselves. At some level we know that the more we focus on the self and our small, singular story, the more lost we can become.

Ironically, it appears that defining happiness from an individual perspective is a relatively modern idea. For thousands of years, human happiness and tribal happiness were synonymous. Happiness was defined as that which was good for the tribe as a whole. It is not that the individual didn't matter, but happiness was mostly the well-being of the greater good.

the thief and the fear of death

It could be argued that the most basic of all human fears is the fear of death. Many of our other phobias, such as of flying, snakes, heights, or others, are often rooted in this more basic fear. The fear of death is, of course, rooted in the focus on the ego and the self as a singular identity separated from the whole. We are afraid to die precisely because we think we exist only as a separate ego identity.

When the Buddha sat under the Bodhi tree to seek enlightenment, part of what he discovered was that the source of all suffering is separation from our true identity. Our true identity is not a separate self but a self that is part of a larger conversation; it began long before we were born in this iteration and will go on long after the death of the body we inhabit. When we become separated from that truth, seeking happiness in the image of our own small ego, unhappiness becomes our companion.

In this regard even our obsession with heaven or an afterlife can be dysfunctional. We are already eternal because we all come from the same source and go back to the same source. Jesus once scolded his followers for their limited thinking when they tried to figure out which wife a man who had several wives might be married to in the afterlife. When we imagine our potential life after death as merely an extension of the ego-bound world we have created for ourselves, we miss our truest nature, which is connection, not separation.

falling out of love with your own story

One of the best proxies for this focus on ego is the way we are wedded to the importance of our own story. Try to be an observer of the way in which many of us talk about our lives. We are obsessed with the story of our own happiness, our journey to discover who we are and why we are here and all the hurts and joys that make up our individual experience. Much of our misery comes when that story of our life does not match some ideal narrative we have about how our life might be.

When I walked the Camino de Santiago, there were many days when I would traverse the Spanish countryside by myself for hours on end. At times I found myself all tied up in knots, thinking about the story of my life. But there were also hours when I refused to talk, not even to myself. Instead of obsessing about my life and where it was headed, I simply stayed in the present moment, connected to everything around me.

Not surprisingly, my happiest moments on the Camino were when I was not thinking about my life story but rather being *in* it without obsessive commentary. The thief loves for us to obsess about our own little story.

Now imagine for a moment an alternative view of the world, which may be very difficult for many. Imagine now that you look up from the pool where you have been staring at your own image, believing it to be the source of happiness and the truth about the world. As you look up, you realize that you are not alone. You are here because of a long line of DNA stretching back far beyond memory or even imagination. In this sense you have always been part of the great lineage of life. Your eternal and connected nature begins to come into your awareness.

You see now that those who have died are alive in you, just as you will be alive in all that comes after you. Your life already has meaning because it is part of a greater story of the revealing of life in the universe. No shortcoming you have, no goal you fail to achieve, no mistake you make on the path of your life story right now—none of this can separate you from the greater conversation of which you are a part. There is nothing you need to do to earn the right to be part of that greater entity, except perhaps to see that because you are part of it, one with it, your life must be used in some way to enhance that greater good. In that moment all fears—of death, of insignificance, of not finding personal happiness—melt into the beauty of the one thing that appears to surround you but of which you are actually a part.

An analogy of our galaxy may be helpful. When you look up on a dark night, far from city lights, you will clearly see a dense constellation of stars that looks like a kind of white film splashed across the sky. The Milky Way appears that way because the galaxy is so dense with stars that their individual lights blend together. It is estimated that there may be 400 billion stars in the galaxy and perhaps 100 billion planets. To the naked eye, the Milky Way appears to be "out there" when, in fact, our solar system is right in its midst. Though it appears that we are outside of it, we are actually inside of it. This is what conceit prevents us from seeing.

We are not separate from other people or from life itself but rather in the very center of it. What appears to be separation is actually an illusion. Quantum physics posits that even time may be an illusion and that everything that has happened and will happen may actually be happening at the same time. As mind-blowing as that may be, it bears witness to the way we can become deluded into believing something to be so true, like time or our ego, even if it simply is not so.

service—the oppositional force

When I interviewed those 250 wise people for *The Five Secrets,* it came as little surprise that most of those identified as happy were not self-focused. Most of them told me that the truest source of happiness was a life of service and a path of giving. All the great teachers have told us this, but most of us ignore it at our own peril. The thief wants us to turn our head toward the water and try desperately to find happiness in our own small ego and its accomplishments, when it knows that lasting happiness can be found only in giving.

Just as the oppositional force of control is surrender, the oppositional force of conceit is *service*. Once again nature can be a great teacher. The biologist Janine Benyus, author of *Biomimicry,* told me once that the purpose in all of nature is to extend life and make it better. This is something the rest of nature appears to remember but that humans can forget. When we are contributing to the greater good, we are in our natural place, connected to our true nature. Most of nature does not have to reflect on its purpose but simply acts in a way to per-petuate and extend life.

Our small ego, that fading image in the pool, will die, but what we contribute to the greater conversation and evolution of life lives on. And we are not doing this for future genera-tions alone. Research has shown that people who consistently perform acts of kindness for others are in fact much happier than those who live more self-oriented lives.[1] As we rise each morning, rather than wonder what the world will give us that day, we might be better to ask, *What can I give the world today?*

Narcissus wanted the image he saw in the pool, but of course each time he reached for it the image faded. So it is with a life lived under the tyranny of conceit. We are always trying to find happiness in the focus on our own small self, when happi-ness can be found only when we look up far enough to see that we are part of a larger story. This is what the Buddha knew. This is what Jesus and all the other great teachers tried to tell us.

In that stillness there is no disturbed water, and we see ourselves for who we truly are.

When I was walking the Camino, some of my happiest moments were when I met someone and felt I was of service to them in some way. This happened numerous times. I vividly recall a young Italian woman in her twenties whom I had met just four days before I finished the journey. She had already walked to Santiago and was now on her way back, which meant several months of walking. We met on a hot afternoon as I noticed her walking in the opposite direction, which was very unusual. When I asked her why, she said, "I am very sick and have been walking the Camino for 40 days; now I am walking back." She held her hand against her abdomen, indicating to me this was the place of her illness. Somehow I knew she had cancer.

For a few short moments, we stood there looking at each other. Something in her eyes conveyed a need to connect. I asked if I could hug her, and she smiled. The short warm embrace connected me to her pain and, I hope, her to my compassion. She looked at me with tears and merely said, "thank you." I never saw her again and am certain I never will, but it was easily one of my happiest moments on the entire trek. In that moment concern about my own happiness and my small ego were absent entirely.

Another experience on the Camino was the realization that thousands of people had walked the same path for 1,200 years. I couldn't help but be aware of the fact that all of those faceless and nameless people were connected to me in the common human quest for purpose. I became deeply aware that the quest itself was bigger than my small part in it. When I finally came to the highest point on the Camino, where people leave rocks brought from home to symbolize something they want to leave behind, I discovered literally thousands and thousands of rocks left over the centuries.

In the presence of so many rocks, there are two potential responses. The thief would want me either to ensure that my rock stood out or to become despondent that my rock was just one among those from so many pilgrims. But the oppositional force—the awareness of my connectedness to all other pilgrims and even to the quest itself—left me smiling. As I put my rock on the pile, I vowed to leave behind my need to be great from an ego standpoint and instead to deeply serve.

I had gone on sabbatical in part to figure out what to do with the rest of my life. The more I walked, the more I became certain that focusing on my own happiness and serving my small ego would not bring me happiness. The thing I needed to give up to find the deepest happiness was separation itself.

kicking the thief out of your house

At this point I hope you see how conceit robs us of our happiness. Now we must follow the same three steps to kick the thief out of the house: notice (catch), stop (arrest), and replace (reform).

Remember that each thief comes in disguise. Conceit is well disguised, making us think that we are separate from others and from life itself. The thief offers us a lovely image in a pool called our ego and tries very hard to convince us that staring at it will bring happiness. This thief is a liar, making us feel separate, alone, and needing to do something to justify our worthiness.

Whenever we find ourselves focused on the happiness of the small self, we must notice this thief. It wants us focused on our small story rather than on the larger narrative of which we have always been a part. In that moment notice the thief, perhaps even with compassion. Most thieves are to be pitied more than loathed. How sad that for so many years this thief has tried so hard to protect the ego, to endeavor to prove its worth, to find a way to differentiate itself from all other things. Have compassion for the part of yourself that feels in exile from everything else.

But compassion does not mean acceptance of the thief's behavior. The thief still must be arrested because it will damage all that it touches. Gently and with no judgment, let the thief know that you have become aware of the larger truth. You are eternal, connected to all that has come before and will come after you. Remind yourself that only when you look up from the small self can happiness be found. Feel the freedom of being a pilgrim on a quest that has a life far beyond you.

Then, of course, replace. What thought pattern or filter might replace conceit? When you find yourself fearing your own death, remind yourself that you are already eternal, already connected to everything that was and will be. It is separation, not connection, that is the illusion. When you think that the key to happiness is falling in love with your own story, remind yourself that only by looking up can we find happiness.

Speak this mantra:

I am connected to all that is; and if I can contribute to the good of the whole, happiness will find me.

Once again, remember that banishing the thieves is a journey akin to learning to mediate or training your muscles. At first it will be difficult, but soon, with practice, it will become who you are.

conceit in society

Conceit and seeing ourselves, or even our species, as the center of the world is detrimental to the future of humanity as well. The wholesale destruction of everything, from the dying coral reefs to the extinction of thousands of species, is driven by humans believing that the world is here for us, rather than our being part of the world. Nature ultimately rewards cooperation rather than conceit and self-focus.

In the late 1960s, Dr. James Lovelock and Dr. Lynn Margulis formulated a theory called the Gaia hypothesis. The idea was that all of planet Earth can be seen as one large organism rather than millions of singular entities. Rather than thinking of the variety of species as being part of earth, all of these species and their sum total relationships are the essence of the earth. This hypothesis posits that without this cooperative interrelationship of all of these organisms, the earth would simply not be the earth as we know it.[2]

Humans are fully a part of nature yet at the same time have a special role in its story. Clearly, we are as dependent on the rest of nature as is any other species because our climate, food, air, and even the basic envelope of life called earth's atmosphere are the result of millions of species interacting. Without this web, human life would cease to exist (and would never have come to be in the first place). To think that everything else that lives and breathes on earth is here only for our benefit is the ultimate conceit.

Although we are part of nature, we clearly have a special role in it. Of all the species on earth, we appear to be the only one capable of looking out into the long future and the distant past to make sense of the path that got us here and to make conscious decisions about the future of life on earth.

It has occurred to me that religious people in the West misinterpreted the Bible when they read in the great myths underlying Western society that we were created in the "image of God." It became a source of conceit when it should have been a source of humility. God or gods, as humans have always imagined them, are creative forces. The nature of God/gods is to create. Being created in the image of God did not make us special; it actually made us more responsible because we were made to create, to bring forth life, to extend and improve the creation.

One of two things is true of humans: we are either in the image of God or are the closest thing to God that we know of. I do not mean we are omnipotent, all powerful, or invincible, or even more important, but that we have the capacity to consider the future and make creative or destructive choices.

Conceit would keep us as humans on a path where, for our own selfish and short-term benefit, we might spoil the great experiment of life on earth. If on the other hand we can reform the thief, to see that the world is not here for us but that we are here for it, perhaps our happiness and the odds of our ultimate survival might improve.

the tribe and the ego

For society the tribe and the species become a proxy for the ego. My tribe and my species may seem somehow like more noble ideas than ego, but they are merely the extension of the ego-based thought pattern that robs us of our happiness. Instead of just me as an entity separate from everything, now we have a collective sense of separation. But because there truly is no "us" or "them," when we allow poverty and suffering to happen to others we in fact are bringing poverty on ourselves. This is the great illusion that this thief so wants us to believe: focus on your family, your tribe, your country, your species, and you will find happiness.

Yet inequality breeds resentment. It fosters the power of hate and anger, and that becomes terrorism or the soil on which mad people like Adolph Hitler can lead humans away from our true nature to a darker side. In truth, when we look up and focus on the well-being of all who surround us—both humans and the natural world—only then can we build a sustainable world for ourselves and future generations.

When we focus only on our own wealth, we create a world in which we must build walls to defend ourselves against those who have less. We erect barriers to keep them out lest they take what is ours, which is ultimately no world that any of us want to live in.

A Mexican friend of mine would often tell me how difficult it was to make a good living in a poor country. Although his family lived well, their home was in an armed, gated community; they feared for their lives on routine shopping trips; and he was robbed twice at gunpoint with his young children by his side. They were wealthy, but the inequality around them meant living in fear. This is the Gaia hypothesis in society: the more we focus on interdependence, on mutual success for all, the more we will create a world where happiness can be ours. If we are willing to sacrifice some of our own wealth to have a society in which there is no extreme poverty, we will benefit as much as those who are less fortunate.

why humans survived

Homo sapiens, as mentioned earlier, were just one of a number of humanlike species that evolved on earth, but we are the only one that survived. The reasons for our ultimate survival are shrouded in mystery, with only scant clues as to why our closest kin like the Neanderthals became extinct and we did not. As the derogatory expression *He's a Neanderthal* shows, the common belief is that *Homo sapiens* survived because we were smarter than our extinct kin. The truth, however, appears to be more complex.

One of the more compelling hypotheses about our ultimate success is the role that myth and story played in the development of cooperation among *Homo sapiens.* We were, by all evidence thus far found, the only humanlike species that created abstract stories and ideas that were able to bind us together to cooperate across large groups of strangers. These early stories involved gods but also beliefs about who we were and our relationship to one another and the rest of the world. Later myths revolved around ideas about democracy or a set of core, commonly held values.

Regardless of the variety of these stories, their purpose was clear: common assent to those stories and myths greased the wheels for us to cooperate and have a sense of tribe even with people we had never met.[3]

humans need a new story

Stories are by all evidence unique to humans. They are powerful and were the prime mode of human communication for millennia. Stories unite but they can also divide. We have fought and continue to fight wars of many kinds over competing stories. An adaptive story can help advance human success, whereas a nonadaptive story can actually compel a species to move itself toward extinction.

Religious stories, also known as myths, have shaped much of human history and continue to do so today. I use the term *myth* but not in the common way it is used by modern society. Most people think of myths as fanciful stories not grounded in fact. Hence we say things like "That is just an urban myth." Here I use *myth* to mean "a shared story within a culture of humans, meant to convey meaning." A myth therefore may be true even without being factual. Its main intent is *not* as historical fact but as conveyer of meaning. To illustrate the power of a common story, we may want to explore one that shaped the relationship the Western world had, and to some extent still has, with nature.

The Hebraic version of creation is a powerful story about who we are as humans. The story is that God created the heavens and the earth in six days. The Koran also says that the world was created in six days, although the word used does not literally mean one day. The sequence of creation is fascinatingly identical to the order in which scientific evidence suggests life evolved. First there was nothing, then came the heavens, then came the earth, then came the creatures of the sea, then those of the land and sky, and finally human beings. This compelling story places humans at the center. We are created last, in the "image of God," and then given "dominion" over all the plants and animals. They are there for our use, and we are in charge.

This is one view of humanity, the story of who we are. We are the exploiters, the species growing at the expense of everything else. We are Narcissus staring at our own image and falling in love with it. We are apart from nature, capturing it for our destiny. Much of the current human condition can be traced to this view of ourselves, regardless of the story that an individual or group might use to source it. In this story we have fulfilled our divinely directed destiny: we have conquered nature and named all the living things of the earth and expropriated them for our own use.

Of course, not all human stories put us at the center of nature. Many aboriginal myths granted to all other creatures the same divine spark found in humans. The animals and plants had as much spirit as we did. Many have posited that the decimation of nature, driven primarily by the European and later North American cultures, was fostered by this core story that placed us at the center of nature and apart from it. We were the only ones with the divine inheritance.

What we had not counted on was that we were never really separate from nature, but very much a part of it. Just as Genesis proposed, we were indeed created last, but seven days was actually billions of years. Even Pope Francis has recently suggested that Catholics ought to believe in evolution. All of nature had to grow, evolve, develop, and mutate until only a moment ago, in evolutionary terms, when we arrived on the scene.

That is why so many people are surprised to discover that the word for having "dominion" in the Jewish creation story is mostly a mistranslation of the original Hebrew word *radah*, which has a royal connotation, so *dominion* meant more like being a king or ruler. The Jewish scriptures later define a good king as one who cares for the people and for the needy. An evil king rules in a way that the people suffer. In this sense the kind of rule the myth suggests we were given over nature is that of a benevolent caretaker; that is, we were granted a special role in nature, as the one who was called to tend the garden.

This is the role that I believe humanity now has the opportunity to reclaim—the chance to be the conscious force of evolution, the force that looks to the future, considers all the living things on earth including ourselves, and chooses a path to sustain the great experiment of life on earth.

Of course, many people in the world hold not a religious view of the source of life but a scientific view of creation. They believe in the big bang, followed by billions of years of evolution and natural selection, which culminated in the world as we know it. Whether we believe we are here by cosmic choice or cosmic chance, humanity needs a unifying story about who we are at this moment in history, a story powerful enough to guide us through this dangerous and opportunistic time in our evolution.

It seems to me that we have spent far too much energy arguing about these two very different belief systems and not nearly enough time exploring how these two fundamentally variant stories lead ultimately to a common meaning for the human journey. We need a unifying story, one that can galvanize concerted action by billions of people.

what a small tribe of hunters can teach humanity

The thief wants us to believe that we are exploiters and selfish by nature. But this is not who we are; it is who we have become under the influence of the thief.

The first hints of a new story came to me in the spring of 2006 while spending time with the Hadza tribe in central Tanzania. Numbering less than a thousand, they are one of the last remaining hunter-gatherer societies in the world. They live, for the most part, the way humans lived for thousands of years before the agricultural revolution. Though they lack almost all of what we consider modern human conveniences, their society has much to teach us.

The Hadza have few material possessions, and almost everything they have is shared. Men and women have different roles (hunting and gathering) but otherwise fairly equal status. There is no permanent or even elected hierarchy. In the history of the Hadza culture, there is no record of famine. Violence among people is very rare.[4]

There are several reasons why there is no record of famine. For one thing, because they have no agriculture and instead depend on hunting and gathering, communities of Hadza move around to follow the food supply. Because the society is communal and sharing is at the core of the culture, whatever food is available is shared. Finally, the nature of hunter-gatherer societies is that they rarely outgrow their ecosystems. Population is thus naturally controlled.

One evening in March 2006, several friends and I sat with about five tribal elders. As the setting sun turned the rock outcroppings bright orange, they began to tell us their creation story. It's a complicated tale involving a giant creature so large that "elephants dangled from his belt." This giant had killed every single person in this part of Africa, save one girl whom he took as his servant. Eventually, this girl fell in love with a man who had sprung from the "honey tree," but the lovers could not be together until they could free themselves from the giant. Soon all the animals of the African plains rose up to help them escape, and from this couple the Hadza tribe was born.

The story was told primarily by one elder named Campolo, but other elders would often chime in to add details. As the story reached its climax, Campolo said that as the young couple ran away from the giant, a huge snake with a blue throat rose up to help them. At this point the elders engaged in a seemingly intense argument about the story that went on for several minutes until Campolo, the oldest of the tribe, continued.

Daude, our main host and translator, was laughing hysterically. When we asked him why, he said, "The elders were arguing about the color of the snake's throat—yellow, black, red, and so on. Finally, Campolo ended the argument, saying, 'What the hell difference does it make? Blue works; it's a story.'"

It reminded me that most of humanity's myths were never meant to be taken quite so literally in terms of the facts. This nuance is lost on most modern followers of religion. Myths are never intended to be read with the mind of a fact checker but rather to convey something far more important than facts: *meaning*.

By the time the elders finished their story, night had fallen. We sat around the campfire with sparks dancing toward a dark sky filled with the beauty of a thousand stars. Soon the elders turned to us, asking to hear *our* creation story.

Because our group of travelers held many different religious and science-based worldviews, we discussed at length which story to tell them—the Garden of Eden, the story from the Hindu scriptures, or the routinely accepted scientific explanation. After much discussion we agreed to tell them the story of the big bang.

For the next 20 minutes, the elders sat rapt as my friend Bill Hawfield, through a translator, told them the scientific creation story. Beginning with the first particle, we waxed a tale: the explosion of the big bang, millions of stars and planets flung out into the universe, the slow cooling of earth, and the emergence of life. First there were the creatures of the sea, some of which crawled onto land, and then the slow evolution from ape to humanity. The first humans had walked not very far from this very spot. Listening to my friend Bill methodically weave the tale of evolution, I couldn't help but think that our story didn't sound much less fantastical than the tale about the giant and the snake with the blue throat.

When we finally finished, the elders discussed our story at length among themselves. They were incredibly animated as they digested our explanation. We waited with great anticipation to hear how these elders would respond to hearing for the first time the accepted scientific explanation of how everything came to be.

After much discussion Daude told us what they made of our story. First, they thought it was a good story, by which they meant a colorful one filled with things you had a hard time imagining. Myths are like that; they are first and foremost good stories. In fact, he said, they liked our story even better than theirs, and he suspected they may have poached their story from another tribe many years earlier.

It was their second response that stopped my breath. They had, they said, figured out the "meaning" of our creation story. They had not listened to the story of the big bang the way a student in a university science class would hear it; they were not interested in the intricacies of natural selection or of the quantum physics behind the molecules that sat before them. They wanted to know what it *meant*. What did the story tell us about who we are?

Their conclusion was simple and profound. The first meaning of the story, they said, is that we humans are connected to all other living things. We exist because they exist. Whatever boundary there is between us and all other creatures is an artificial one.

They also concluded that the story tells us that we are important, that humans play a critical role in the evolution of life. We have been given the responsibility of caring for the creation. It struck me that they had used the word *important* rather than *special.* To be special is to be above nature (to stare at one's own image in the pool), but to be important is to have a role that matters in relationship to all of creation. As discussed earlier, it can be argued that the purpose of all nature is to extend life and make it better.

humanity's collective search for happiness

This is the heart of the challenge we face as humans. We have at times felt insignificant and at other times special, but we have rarely grasped our place in the course of evolution. It occurred to me that night, sitting by the fire and later dancing with the Hadza elders, that the facts of science can sometimes cause us to lose sight of the more important questions. If the accepted scientific explanation of the big bang and evolution are true, what do they tell us about who we are and what our relationship is to the earth?

It seems to me that the lessons of this emerging myth are several. First, if humans are the culmination, thus far, of 4 billion years of evolution on earth, then we exist—we ride—firmly on the back of the rest of the biosphere. We have come to exist at the end of a long, complicated chain of life. When we refer to "Mother Earth," it is no mere turn of phrase; we exist because of all the other creatures that came before us. Without them we would not be here. Whatever we are and whatever is unique about us, the other creatures of the planet are not here merely for our use but have lives and purposes of their own—a life in almost all cases more ancient than our own.

Our individual lifespan is very short in the context of this larger story. In the context of several billion years, we do indeed live in a borrowed world, one that is ours for a very brief time. But does this make us more or less relevant? If we are in the midst of billions of years of evolution, with billions of years yet to go, perhaps the story tells us that what we do to the world in our lifetime means little. After all, we are but bit players in a long, perhaps endless play.

Perhaps. Yet there is another interpretation of this emerging story, one that could forever change our view of ourselves as humankind.

What if planet Earth is the only place in the entire universe where intelligent life is found? What if this is the one outcropping of sentient life in the vast and infinite universe? What if, after billions of years of evolution, only once in the history of the universe did a planet such as this emerge from the remnant? There may be, or may have been, thousands of other civilizations in the universe, but so far as we know this is the only place where the cosmos is reflecting on itself.

It does not really matter if you are a humanist or a believer in God (or gods), or force, or cosmic consciousness. Either way you see the world, we are unique, but not in the way we thought we were—special, gifted, entitled. Rather we are unique because we are conscious. If we can move away from our conceit, we can become a positive, creative force for the future of the experiment of life. In that process our individual lives will be filled with meaning as we do our part in the short time we have to join that larger dance. By looking up from the pool where a false image promises happiness, our entire species we will find meaning in serving the oneness of which we are a part.

a life without conceit

Conceit is a powerful thief, focusing us on our small ego. Like Narcissus we will find ourselves forever reaching for happiness where it cannot be found in the pursuit of the self, ultimately leaving us to spiritually die from exhaustion. Should we choose to keep the thief at bay, we can claim our rightful place as part of a story larger than ourselves that is, itself, eternal. In that sur-render we come to see that serving the greater good is the path to happiness. It comes only when we stop worrying about our own story and join the grand conversation all around us. All of humanity must also tame the thief, lest we destroy the very bio-sphere that gave us life, the complex system of which we have never been separate but in which we have a special opportunity to serve.

Even death, which robs many people of happiness, melts away once the veil of separation is lifted. What is the fear of death if not the fear of loss of our conceit, the fear that we are not important outside our context within the whole? Once we see what is actually true—that there is no true separation between ourselves and anything "out there"—this thief no lon-ger has the power to exploit our fear of not being unique, or special, or distinct.

four ways to banish the second thief

- Whenever you find yourself obsessing about the story of your life, remind yourself that you are already a part of a larger story. The thief wants you sitting around, staring at your reflection, but there is no happiness to be found there.

- Remember that happiness is a by-product of being a part of something larger than yourself—a cause, a life's work, or service to nature or other people. Focus on serving rather than on receiving.

- When the fear of death looms, tell yourself that it is a lie. You in some form have been here since time began and will be here for all time. The image in the water is not real, just as time itself may not be.

- In our common life, let us join together in a new myth that can unite those of faith and of science. Humans are part of nature but have a special role in nature. As caretakers of the great experiment of life, we can find collective meaning. Building an equitable world that works for all is part of this, if not for moral reasons then for practical ones. Only when all prosper can we all be truly safe and happy.

mantra

I am connected to all that is; and if I can contribute to the good of the whole, happiness will find me.

chapter four

the third thief: coveting

I grew up going to Sunday school in a Christian church.

Among the things that were drilled into our young minds were the Ten Commandments, supposedly given by God directly on two stone tablets to the Jewish leader Moses atop Mt. Sinai. Among those commandments is: "You shall not covet your neighbor's house. You shall not covet your neighbor's wife, or his male or female servant, his ox or donkey, or anything that belongs to your neighbor."[1]

To covet is to desire, with envy, something for yourself that you do not have. This commandment always seemed out of place to me, nested as it was with what seemed like much more serious offences such as stealing, killing, and lying. Even more strikingly, the other nine commandments pertained to external acts, but this one was an admonition against an internal state of mind. Even as a young boy, sitting there on Sunday mornings, I wondered if wanting something could really be as serious as stealing or murdering someone.

Coveting is another powerful thief. It is tricky in many ways because it comes disguised as something that may seem harmless or even ambitious in some productive way. What could be wrong with wanting to have something you don't yet possess? Is not desire for something the very source of moving forward in life? Once we look closely at coveting, however, we soon realize why it is such an effective thief of happiness.

Coveting is not just about wanting something; it combines several elements that undermine our happiness. Coveting is not just everyday desire; it is the part of us that looks out at what others have, or at something we don't have, and brings back on ourselves a feeling of envy. Envy is the sense of discontentment or even resentful longing, often aroused by someone else's qualities, possessions, or luck. When we see that coveting is as much about what we allow ourselves to feel inside as it is about the object of outward desire, its role in stealing happiness becomes apparent.

Think about all the things many of us covet that we don't have: for more money, for higher status, for our natural gifts to be different from the ones we were bestowed with, for our spouses or partners to be different, for our hair to be a different texture, for our height to be shorter or taller, for us to be younger or older than we are, and the list goes on. The thief is always telling us that we should be in a place of deficit, disappointment, and envy. At its core, this thief is constantly telling us that our sense of self comes from reference to the outside world, focused on the question *How do I compare?*

the wicked queen in *snow white*

This thief is much like the wicked queen in the well-known fairy tale *Snow White*. Snow White's mother died in childbirth and her father, the king, remarried. The new queen was beautiful, but her happiness could be found only in comparison with others. Each day she asked the magic mirror that now infamous question: *Mirror, mirror, on the wall, who is the fairest of them all?* The queen was happy so long as the mirror told her that she was fairer than any other. One day the mirror told her that while she was indeed beautiful, Snow White was yet fairer. Not only did the thief send her into a rage, ruining her internal contentment, but it also ruined her relationship with the outer world, as she sent the huntsman out to kill Snow White.

This is what coveting does. It takes away our capacity to be grateful, not only for ourselves but also for others. This is a critical point about coveting: It infects our personal happiness, but it also undermines our relationships with others. Instead of celebrating and sharing in the happiness of others, we resent their happiness and good fortune.

The thief may even feed antisocial behavior. *Air rage* is the general term for disruptive or violent behavior perpetrated by passengers and crew of aircraft, typically during flight, and the phenomenon is occurring with growing frequency on commercial flights around the world. A recent study showed a significant correlation between instances of air rage and whether there was a first-class cabin on the aircraft. There were significantly more air-rage incidents when there was a discrepancy between those in coach and those in more-comfortable seats. Even more fascinatingly, the researchers found that on airplanes with both first-class and economy cabins, rage was significantly lower if there were separate entrances for each cabin; that is, if those in economy class did not have to see the first-class cabin, there was less rage. Although the researchers grant that there could be many alternative explanations for their findings, it is not hard to imagine the thief's role in instigating this antisocial behavior.[2]

This may also help explain why levels of happiness and trust are often higher in countries where there is more equality. A psychologist friend of mine is originally from Denmark. She told me that when she was growing up, she felt that most everyone was pretty equal in terms of income, so it seemed to her that people were generally more content. In their book *The Spirit Level: Why Greater Equality Makes Societies Stronger,* Richard Wilkinson and Kate Pickett explore this very idea—that more-equal societies do better. They share research showing that on 11 different health and societal issues, such as physical health, mental health, violence, obesity, imprisonment, and teenage pregnancies, outcomes are significantly worse in societies with greater inequality, regardless of whether the country is rich or poor.[3]

Although creating a more equitable society is a noble and important goal, my point is that when people feel that they are more or less on an even playing field with others, it appears to not set off our coveting tendency. Yet a completely equitable society is not possible. Even if income were completely equal, there would always be differences in other aspects, such as intelligence, athletic ability, conventional beauty, height, weight, the qualities of your parents, and so on. Although one way to keep the thief in check would be to try to surround ourselves with people who are less or only as fortunate as we are, it seems that an easier path would be to work on our own inner life so that we can enjoy the success of others without becoming less happy ourselves.

gratitude—the oppositional force

The oppositional force of coveting is *gratitude*. Recent research has shown the incredible power of gratitude to increase our sense of well-being and happiness, to improve our health, to help us age well, and even to foster prosocial behavior.

Robert Emmons, a professor at the University of California, Davis, is a pioneer in research on gratitude. In some of his seminal work, he and his colleagues randomly put people in one of three conditions. The first group was asked to journal about five things they were grateful for from the previous week, a second group was asked to journal about five things that irritated them in the previous week, and a final control group was asked to simply journal about five events from the previous last week with no further instruction. The research demonstrated that by the end of the study, those who journaled about gratitude were less stressed and more optimistic and reported on average being 25 percent happier than the other participants. It also turned out that they exercised more and reported fewer health problems. Over time the research included people who were experiencing disease, and the researchers demonstrated that even people in difficult life situations experienced significant gains in happiness, optimism, and pain reduction through the simple act of journaling about gratitude. Interestingly, those who practiced such journaling also reported being kinder and more supportive of others.

In one particularly revealing study, Emmons identified people who had strong dispositions toward gratitude. The researchers then asked friends of these people to complete a survey about them, comparing these responses to similar responses from friends of less grateful people. According to the friends, grateful people engaged in more supportive, kind, and helpful behaviors (e.g., loaning money or providing compassion, sympathy, and emotional support) than did less grateful people.[4]

A growing body of research on the benefits of gratitude has been piling up since Emmons and a few others pioneered this line of inquiry. In a recent *Psychology Today* blog, author Ann Morin summarized much of that research and identified seven benefits.[5] Among those now-proven benefits, she says, are that grateful people experience fewer aches and pains, they are more likely to exercise, they are happier and less depressed, they are more likely to behave in prosocial ways, and they sleep better, have higher self-esteem, and are more resilient in the face of stressful situations. Grateful people are also less likely to want to retaliate or be aggressive toward others when given negative feedback. There is even compelling evidence that gratitude boosts the immune system!

What is truly noteworthy is that in most of these studies, some people had more to objectively be grateful for than did others. Many of us tend to think we would be happier if we were more fortunate. Yet this research suggests that gratitude, the oppositional force of coveting, can be nurtured by simple daily practices such as journaling about that for which we are grateful. In other words, because people were randomly assigned to focus on gratitude, what we objectively have to be grateful for is not nearly as important as the mind-set that we cultivate toward whatever we do have.

Cultivating that mind-set might mean journaling not only about what we are grateful for but also about instances of good fortune that befall those around us. It seems that by cultivating this mind-set toward others as well, we might reduce our coveting habit. I have been journaling about gratitude for some time now and have found it to be a high-impact habit for my happiness.

what is success?

Expressing gratitude by itself is not enough to tame the thief, however. To banish the thief, we must learn to live by our own compass rather than someone else's. The thief wants us to judge our success in life by the answer from the magic mirror, by looking out and comparing ourselves with others instead of focusing on our own path.

Years ago a 100-year-old woman named Lucy admonished me to never compare myself with others because everyone has different gifts. The thief always wants us to believe that what we need is what someone else has. We become like a cartoon I saw years ago that featured four cows at the intersection of four farms, each with her head stretched across the fence to eat the grass on another farm. We always think what someone else has is what we need to be happy.

Here is a personal example of how coveting can focus us on the wrong things. I have loved sports my entire life, having grown up in a neighborhood full of boys, where sports were the major source of identity. I would have loved to have been six foot four with great athletic ability, but I am five foot seven with average athletic ability. As a child, I coveted the athletic prowess of the neighbor boys who had it, and that robbed me of much happiness, even causing me to diminish the gifts I did have. This attitude also separated me from enjoying the other boys' successes because my coveting of their skill would not allow me to fully celebrate them without diminishing myself. My best friend's older brother was a high-school baseball star with the potential to be drafted to the major leagues. With embarrassment I now admit that I once secretly rooted for him to lose a big game that I was watching. Here was a person whom I liked and admired, and there I was, rooting for him to fail!

The thief not only made me miserable but kept me from truly celebrating others' good fortune. When we live our life in comparison with others, like the wicked queen did with Snow White, we not only find ourselves unhappy but we cannot share the joy of others because their happiness makes us feel less good about ourselves.

This may help explain the rather common angst that people often feel on social media sites such as Facebook and Instagram. Some research studies have suggested an inverse relationship between use of social media and happiness. A study in Denmark by the Happiness Institute demonstrated increases in happiness when people stop using Facebook for two weeks. The study suggests that envy or coveting may be the key cause of this inverse relationship.[6] Looking at the postings of others, we may find ourselves asking, *Who has the most interesting life of all, the most friends of all, and the most likes of all?* The thief wants us to always be looking over to see what our neighbor, our co-worker, and the family down the road or across the city has instead of what we have.

Even more interestingly, some studies have found the opposite to be true: that time on social media increases social connection, enhances political activism, reduces stress, and builds stronger relationships.[7] So why the discrepancy? It turns out that the very thief we are discussing is at play.

It appears that what we do on social media greatly influences how it makes us feel. A 2010 study from Carnegie Mellon[8] found that when people engaged with others in direct interaction, such as posting on walls, messaging others, supporting mutual causes, and "liking" something, their feelings of bonding and general social capital increased while their sense of loneliness decreased. But when participants simply consumed a lot of content passively, social media had the opposite effect, lowering their feelings of connection and increasing their sense of loneliness.

Let me take an educated guess as to why this might be the case. When we mostly view what others are doing, as mere witnesses to their happy moments and successes, we hear the thief telling us that our life does not compare. When we come from a place of gratitude, however, engaging, celebrating, and connecting with others, we become happier.

The thief can show up in ways that are almost embarrassing to admit. These small moments of coveting are an opportunity to practice for the larger things. I experienced this when a friend of mine posted pictures of herself sleeping in tents in the Moroccan Sahara. It had been I who recommended that she take this particular excursion because of a similar experience I had had the year before. Quickly, I noticed that she had a lot more likes from her pictures then I had when mine were posted. The thief tapped me on the shoulder. "Be unhappy," it said. The thief didn't want me to like her photos or comment on them in a positive way. But I resisted the thief, and not only liked her photos but sent her a very positive comment to which she gave a warm and gracious reply. I felt more connected, enjoyed her moment of happiness, and felt happier myself. If instead I had listened to the thief, I would surely have felt worse about my life and missed an opportunity to make my friend happier, as well.

Even in situations when we are competing with others, the thief does not serve us well. A friend of mine was trying out for a sports team and felt she was surely better than another player who was also trying out. She said to the coach, "How is she better than me?"

The coach said, "Stop worrying about the other players and just focus on being the best player you can be."

My friend said this comment shifted something inside her. Did she really want to make the team because someone else didn't do well? She decided to start praying for and rooting for the success of the other players, including the person she had derided to the coach. She even decided to help pay for a stronger young player who was trying out for the same position she played, who could not afford to do so. Not only did she enjoy the tryout process more but she took her eyes off what others were doing to focus on her own game. She found herself playing much better, with the thief relegated to the bench.

big dogs, little dogs, and happy dogs

One of my mentors early in my life told me that when you spend your life comparing yourself with others, you will always find yourself feeling like a Chihuahua among Saint Bernards. Simply translated, there will always be a dog bigger than you or who has qualities you wish you had. Instead of celebrating the dog you are, you will always find yourself wishing you were another breed.

This thief is a trickster. It comes disguised as helpful ambition, focusing us to achieve and grow, but then it tricks us by making the reference point for happiness how we compare with others instead of whether we are being ourselves or developing our gifts to our best capacity. Life becomes a contest instead of a journey.

This became real to me when I published my first book. It was a great accomplishment, and I thought for certain that once it was published my heart would be filled with gratitude. But suddenly instead of comparing myself with those who had never written a book, I compared myself with those who had written multiple books. Then when my first book became a best seller, instead of being filled with gratitude, I found myself focusing on those whose books were mega–best sellers. Whatever happiness writing a book had brought me was stolen when the thief had me comparing myself with others instead of focusing on what I had accomplished.

The thief keeps us asking the wrong question. Instead of asking who we are, we find ourselves focusing on how we compare. The great task of life is not to be better than others but to truly be ourselves. When I wrote *The Five Secrets,* many of the people I interviewed warned me about comparing ourselves to others, but even more profoundly they told me that the great task of life was to *be yourself!* That is, to know what makes you happy and to live by that internal compass rather than by what others tell you matters. How we compare is a question that will never have a positive answer because either the mirror will tell us that someone else is fairer or we will have to keep checking in with the mirror every day to make sure we haven't lost our spot! It is hard to imagine a more exhausting life than one forever lived in comparison with others.

A magazine editor asked me years ago to write a 1,500-word essay on the theme *What matters most?* A group of compelling personalities were all taking a crack at that question, and I felt honored (and intimidated) to participate. It also felt a bit daunting to forever put down on paper my view of what mattered most. For weeks I racked my brain. What matters most—love, world peace, spirituality, health, relationships, family, legacy? The list seemed infinite. In the end my essay posited a simple idea: what matters most is to know what matters most to *you* and to live your life focused on that.

This is exactly why the third thief can be so dangerous. If we live our life comparing ourselves with others, we can easily find ourselves climbing up a long ladder to the top of a building we aren't even sure we want to be on. When we look in the mirror, rather than ask how we compare, we should be asking questions like *What do I value? What matters to me? What is the best use of my one life?*

banishing the thief

Now that we are aware of the impact this thief has on our happiness, we must be intentional about banishing it. Once again, the three steps become an essential tool. Aware now of the thief, you will start to notice its presence on a regular basis. It will show up even in simple daily circumstances like when a colleague or friend comes to work looking particularly good or when something positive happens in the life of someone you know. It will show up on your best days, when you realize that what you accomplish never seems to be enough for you, and also on your worst days, when you find it hard to connect to gratitude. Remember that in meditation the goal is always to gently brush aside thoughts that do not serve us.

Begin to notice the thief's presence with a sense of humor, if you can. Imagine yourself saying, *Now there you go again, comparing yourself with others.* The act of noticing may not seem like a powerful force, but it is. The first step in all matters of the mind is to see what is really going on. Noticing and naming something often goes a long way toward disarming it. When I found myself noticing the thief when my friend posted those Facebook pictures of her trip to the desert, that alone was enough to shift my emotion and thinking. When another friend launched a new online leadership program with success and I felt a hint of coveting, just by becoming aware of it I was able to brush it aside and move into a place of gratitude for her.

Once a thief loses its disguise, it can't trick you any further. It's like the moment you find out the secret behind a magic trick. Suddenly, the trick, or even a similar one, can't fool you anymore, even if you wanted it to. Try to become adept at identifying the thief's disguises. The more you uncover it, the better your mind will become at disarming the thief before it even triggers your reaction.

Once we notice the thief, of course, we must stop or arrest it. Stopping is an act of imposing our will on the thief. Every time we refuse to give the thief power, it loosens its grip on us. A thief that is arrested every time will eventually stop trying. This is an important point to remember. There is solid science behind the idea that every time we stop something, we are less likely to do it again.

Alvaro Pascual-Loene, the noted Harvard neuroscientist referenced earlier, told me once, "Every time we do something from a brain perspective, we are more likely to do it again; but every time we *don't* do something, we are less likely to do it next time. It creates a path of habit that becomes the pattern of your life."

The act of simply stopping something, of refusing to let it dominate your mind, is an act of great significance. There is a wonderful old video on YouTube where the comedian Bob Newhart plays a therapist doing a session with a new patient who has a phobia about being buried alive in a box.[9] As she tells him all the reasons she has this phobia, he gives her a simple piece of advice: "Stop it!" She continues to provide rationales for her fear, but he repeats, "Just stop it!" Eventually, she brings up more problems, such as destructive relationships with men and a fear of driving. Each time he simply says, "Stop it!" He reminds her how unhealthy this way of thinking is for her. She becomes more and more agitated as he keeps telling her to "stop it."

Finally, she says, "I don't like this! I don't like this therapy at all. You're just telling me to stop it!"

There is a part of us that resists the idea that we are quite capable of reprogramming our minds. The banishing of the thieves always starts with those two words: *Stop it!* If you start to compare yourself with others—you got it—just stop it.

As always, replacing is the key third step. We need a new thought pattern to take over from the coveting orientation. In this case, the replacement is to remind yourself that life is not a contest. Our worth as a human being is not about how we compare with others but about truly living to our own best potential. We cannot control how we compare with others.

The new thought pattern can best be expressed in this mantra:

Life is not a contest. I will be grateful for what I have and who I am. I will celebrate the success of others; for when I celebrate for others, I am happy.

Practice this mantra, not only when the thief is present but also when the thief is not in the room. The best time to disarm a thief is before it becomes active, and these mantras are a great way to prevent the thief from even showing up. Think of the mantras as a kind of a metal detector for the mind. We want to program our mind ahead of time so that the thief never gets into the house in the first place. Catching and arresting a thief can work, but it sure is a lot easier to thief-proof your house.

the coveting society

This thief also infects our community life. It doesn't really matter whether you believe that the Ten Commandments were given to Moses by God or that they represent the collective wisdom of ethical behavior among Jews in ancient times, but it's worth pondering why coveting sat alongside seemingly more egregious acts like lying, stealing, and killing another person. Could coveting truly be a destructive force in society rather than a harmless personal envy that robs us of our happiness?

The reason coveting is in the company of these more heinous acts is subtle. If I look at my neighbors' possessions and qualities with coveting as the dominant force, the very sentiment in my heart is the forerunner to feeling that I have the right to take what they have or do what I want to them, even if it causes them harm. Thoughts of envy or desire for something we don't have are natural and in and of themselves harmless. But when we indulge those thoughts long enough, when we let them become the dominant way we see others, it makes the actual act of betrayal more likely to occur. Coveting is then the precursor of the action we know to be destructive for the community. Stopping the thief at the door is the key to preventing the antisocial behavior.

Research on gratitude suggests that being in a place of gratitude—celebrating our place in the world rather than coveting another place—increases our empathy, kindness, and desire to support others. The opposite is also true: when we are in a place of coveting, we find ourselves acting out toward others.

Let me use a personal example that I think illustrates what can happen when we are not in a place of gratitude. I am generally considered to be a kind person, and this is something I am proud of. All of my life, it has been important to me to be nice to others, even strangers who will encounter me only once. One night I was in the middle of a busy week, catching a flight that would arrive at 1 a.m. to do an entire day session with a colleague at the office of a large client of mine. Just before my flight took off, I got a voice mail from the person who was supposed to do the full-day session with me. He was apologizing that, because of a family illness, I would need to lead the session by myself.

Though I felt compassion for my colleague, I wanted things to be different. I was tired and didn't want to do the all-day session with what I knew would be a tough group. Instead of being grateful that I could support him, I focused on my desire for things to be different. As I got on the plane, this normally kind guy was very rude with the flight attendants and then almost nasty as I pushed past the person in the aisle seat to take my place by the window. As we took off, I reflected with some embarrassment on my behavior. This in miniature is what coveting does. Whenever I want things to be different, somehow I feel cheated. That resentment wells up, and my behavior is less gracious.

But so what if a normally kind person is a little rude because he is not in a place of gratitude? Does this really have an impact on society? It seems to me that it does—and maybe in more pervasive ways than we might first imagine. A wealthy couple who live in a society where others are not so fortunate will likely not resent paying more in taxes if they are focused on gratitude for what they have, rather than needing to covet even more. Popular high-school students might be more compassionate to those who are bullied if they focused on how grateful they are for their often-unearned popularity, rather than coveting someone else's even greater popularity. It might prevent a young man from vandalizing a nice car in a more affluent neighborhood, in part because he resents that driver's relative wealth. A country blessed by natural resources and a relatively homogenous society might feel more compelled to help other nations that are not so fortunate if they were to focus on the good fortune that gave them their home of relative safety and comfort.

What's more, history is filled with examples of tyrants who used the third thief to turn one tribe against another. Think of how Adolf Hitler used the success of German Jews in business to foster resentment among people who had no reason to hate the Jews. This always begins in subtle ways and soon becomes dangerous.

This is not to say that gratitude is a panacea or that coveting is the source of all evils. But the emerging research on the relationship between gratitude and prosocial behavior suggests that when we focus on what we have, instead of on what we don't have, we wind up being kinder, more willing to share, and less likely to retaliate. It is therefore not much of a stretch to imagine that a world in which the covetous thief has been banished would be kinder than the one we now inhabit.

ambition is good; comparison robs you

The third thief is a subtle one. Ambition is good, and so is the desire to improve ourselves. But when we allow our life to be about comparison with others, we soon find ourselves in an endless search for a happiness we'll never find. Someone else will always have more friends, be more beautiful, and possess gifts we wish we had. Not only will our own happiness be ruined but we will be unable to celebrate the success of others. Instead of asking the mirror, *Who is the fairest of them all?* we must ask, *Am I being myself? Have I truly become all that I am capable of and meant to be?*

four ways to banish the third thief

- Whenever you find yourself asking the mirror on the wall of your subconscious how you compare with others, remember that it is the thief speaking to you. It is lying when it tells that you that life is a contest rather than a journey. Ask instead: *Am I being my best self?*

- Practice gratitude through daily journaling or simply taking a few minutes to identify three things that you are grateful for in that day and one in your life. Each day choose another person and write down three things you want to celebrate for them.

- When using social media, focus on adding value to others' interactions, engaging with them and showing your happiness for them. Once this muscle is flexed, you will see that happiness comes from this and not from coveting.

- Remember that there will never be full social equality in all matters. Others are rarely responsible for our unhappiness. Tame the coveting spirit inside yourself to better the world around you. Whenever there is a chance to help someone less fortunate, focus on your gratitude as a source of kindness.

mantra

Life is not a contest. I will be grateful for what I have and who I am. I will celebrate the success of others; for when I celebrate for others, I am happy.

chapter five

the fourth thief: consumption

Years ago I had an assistant named Janice, who was an incredibly bright light, a warm human being, and a frequent reader of self-help material. One day she was sitting at her desk with a quizzical look on her face. Turning toward her, I asked, "What are you thinking about?"

"I was just sitting here thinking of all the things we try to do to make ourselves happy," she said. "Find a relationship, make money, take up hobbies, get more friends, and so on. Then it occurred to me, *What if one day we just decided to be happy instead?*"

We went about our day, but that comment ran around for days in my head like a virus I couldn't shake. *What if,* I wondered, *happiness were not out there at all, in anything we did or did not do, nor in anything we received or did not receive? What if happiness were a choice, more or less available to us at any moment we chose to be in that internal state?*

The fourth thief is named *consumption*—the one that tells us that there is something outside ourselves that we need to achieve happiness, and it tries to hide from us the truth that we can choose it at any moment. Intuitively, of course, we all know that happiness cannot come from consumption of something because we all know people who appear to "have it all" but are consistently discontent, as well as people who have "next to nothing" and appear to be quite happy. This thief is like a thirsty person with a large bottle of good, fresh water but a hole in their throat. In the Buddhist tradition, there is a concept of the soul as a "hungry ghost," a spirit that is always seeking something, but no matter what it finds, that soul is still hungry.

This thief constantly whispers an insidious mantra in your ear that goes something like "If and when you have *x*, you will be happy." You can fill in the blank: *I would be truly happy if I had…* a nicer house, a better spouse, more external success, a new body, a best seller, more Facebook friends, a remodeled house, more followers on Twitter, more fame or less fame, more leisure time or more work, and so on.

Don't be fooled that this is about consumption in the way we normally think of it. We normally think of consumption as buying things. This thief is far trickier than that. This thief tells us that happiness is *out there*.

Happiness is a choice. This is the truth that this thief tries so hard to hide from us.

the man who lost the key

There is a wonderful story in the Sufi tradition that truly shows us who this thief is.

A man was walking home late one night when he saw his friend Mulla on his hands and knees under a street light, obviously searching for something.

"Mulla, what have you lost?" he asked.

"The key to my house."

"I'll help you look," the friend said. "Where exactly did you drop it?"

"Over there, inside my house."

"Then why are you looking for it here?"

"Because there is more light here."

The story borders on the ludicrous at first reading, something like an old vaudeville joke, until you place the fourth thief as the main protagonist. Mulla represents all of us looking outside of our own house for that which cannot be found there. We look for happiness outside ourselves because the thief has made us believe that it is easier to find something outside. The work inside the house is more difficult, but because it is the place where happiness ultimately lies, inside we must go.

In my daily meditation, I always end with a mantra. My personal mantra, spoken numerous times during my meditation each day, begins with the words *I choose contentment.* These words were selected very carefully. The word *contentment* was chosen because I believe that it is not always possible to choose to feel happy, but we *can* choose to be content. Contentment, the decision to accept things as they are at that very moment, is really a choice not to be "unhappy." Whenever I find myself feeling unhappy, I repeat to myself, *I choose contentment.*

When I shared this idea with a stranger recently, he told me that it brought him immediate relief. He said, "I get it. Whatever is happening at any moment, I have the power to choose not to be unhappy. Contentment does not mean a smiley face; it does mean a decision to choose to be at peace."

the happiness choice

Consumption, of course, is at the root of our entire consumer society, and we have sadly built an economic system based on each of us believing that we need to buy something to have contentment. Ads ask us to "open happiness" with a bottle of Coke, as if happiness required us to open anything up. Dating sites promise that happiness is just one lunch date away. Our old car may work just fine, but look how happy these people seem behind the wheel of a brand-new car. I think it is no accident that the "hungry ghost" society we have built is literally destroying the planet as a result of our never-ending search for happiness out there.

This thief even plays havoc with the most basic of human endeavors: relationships. The thief deceives us into thinking that the source of happiness is to consume love, that we will be happy if we get others to love us. In fact, love—the love of the self—is already ours to possess without anything outside ourselves. The choice to be a loving person and to act with love toward every person we meet is already within our power. Ironically, it is often those most filled with self-love—and who act with love toward others—who attract love to themselves. It is those who are most focused on being loved, on seeking others' approval, on "consuming love," whom we often find to be the least loveable. Getting love is not the secret to happiness, but *becoming* love *is* one such secret.

The idea that happiness is a choice, one that we can make at any moment, is so simple and radical that we often resist it. We have been so conditioned to think of happiness as a by-product of something else that when I tell people they should *choose* to be content, many get somewhat irritated. To be honest, sometimes it even irritates me when I remind myself of it! Watch how you feel when reminded that contentment is a choice that you can simply make at any time. Notice the way the thief tries to lie to you, claiming that it is something to be acquired.

It's not that we can't or shouldn't take pleasure in things or people outside ourselves. Sunshine is pleasurable to me, but the choice to be unhappy and discontent when it is raining is my own. Taking a nice vacation brings pleasure, but the choice to be unhappy upon returning home is simply that—a choice. Having a great relationship is a source of joy, but the idea that one cannot be happy without a relationship is a lie. The thief tells me that when it is sunny, when I am on vacation, and when I have a relationship, *then* I will be happy.

As with all the thieves, the key to showing them out of the house of your life is to be mindful of them. It is to notice, without judgment of self or even of the thief, the way each thief shows up as you go about your day. When it is raining and the thief whispers to you, "If only it were sunny," you can gently observe its presence and brush it aside.

Happiness and contentment are products of the mind. This is why Shakespeare famously put these words in the mouth of Hamlet: "for there is nothing either good or bad, but thinking makes it so."[1] This simple knowledge is life-changing but rarely accepted. Happiness is not in what is happening; it is in how I *process* what is happening.

But if happiness is a choice, does that mean that feelings of sadness are not natural? Are feelings of sadness the same as unhappiness? Is the definition of a good, worthy, well-lived human life one in which we are always in a happy mood?

We now know that some people have physiological conditions that make it more difficult to regulate mood, and, of course, for these people we are discovering new treatments to help. Some in my own family have benefited from this, and there is no shame in taking medicines that can help balance one's moods. But the techniques described here that help us choose happiness are still relevant, even if you are one of those people.

It would not surprise me if one day there is a happiness pill available to all that will stimulate the brain to emit happiness chemicals at our command. Why should we even bother to learn to tame the thieves when there is, or one day will be, a drug to make all of us feel happy all the time?

This is an important and even deep query, as it raises the question of whether sadness, grief, and sorrow are valuable human emotions. Is a good human life one in which we never experience those things? Perhaps a full human life is one in which even these unhappy emotions are embraced, not as externalities to be overcome but as opportunities for us to claim our human capability to choose contentment even amid "negative" emotions?

Even here the thief lies to us. It tells us not only that happiness is out there but that negative emotions and sadness are the enemy. They may be unpleasant at times, but they are not the enemy. If we define happiness only as the happy feeling when all is going well, we miss a significant part of what it means to be human. The choice to be content can occur even in sad times rife with negative emotions.

Research suggests that some of the emotions we consider negative actually serve a positive evolutionary survival benefit. Researchers at the University of New South Wales in Australia found that sadness actually increases motivation, perseverance, and generosity.[2] To be an enlightened human being is to master the world of your mind—to be able to rise above even the sad emotions that come to us and choose contentment. Every unhappy event is a way to discover again the truest spiritual journey, which is to choose our state of consciousness. This we have in our power, but like all powers it must be trained and disciplined.

i will be happy if...

The mind is like any muscle: the more we exercise it, the more it strengthens. A simple practice is to become fully aware anytime you find yourself thinking *I will be happy if…* or *I will be happy when…* These two phrases are a clue that the thief is in the house. It doesn't much matter what comes after those phrases because the words that follow will not make you happy. Better said, you don't require them to choose happiness and contentment.

Whenever you find yourself thinking *if* and *when,* replace that filter with this simple mantra:

> *I can choose happiness and contentment right now. It is a product of my mind, not a result of what is happening. Right now I will choose happiness.*

At first you will have to do this many times. It will seem to be merely a mental exercise as your untrained mind objects. But it is the thief who is objecting. Your wiser self already knows the truth. The only way to be rid of a thief is not to let it invade your house. First you must banish it, and eventually it will realize that it's not welcome, at least not in your house.

It sounds simple; it is. It seems like it will take patience to reprogram your mind; it will. Once you master it, however, happiness is there for you, always.

consumption in society

This thief is also robbing humanity both in the present moment and the future. We must see that the same hungry ghost that keeps us trying to find happiness *out there* as individuals is part of what keeps the whole society consuming without any true connection to the consequences of that consumption. I am not against consumption nor averse to nice things, new technology, or a nice new pair of shoes. But an entire economic system that requires us to consume constantly or risk the whole thing unraveling is one that is controlling us more than we are controlling it. This is as dysfunctional for the entire species as it is for an individual human being.

We recently moved into a new home. As we prepared to move, we realized how many clothes, shoes, and possessions we had accumulated over the years that we have hardly ever used. Many items of clothing were worn once and never again. Thinking back on some of those items, it occurs to me that many of them were purchased in a moment when the thief was with me in the store. I may have been unhappy and felt like I needed something new to bring me happiness. Of course, the new thing didn't deliver on its promise.

Our new home is a duplex that we share with another couple. Living in half a home, with another couple right next door, I couldn't help but think about our society's focus on possession. It begins when we are very young, as we cry aloud to another child, "That is *my* toy!" The thief reinforces our sense of isolation and loneliness. We become obsessed with *my* and *mine* rather than *ours* and *we*. I started thinking about how many duplicate items there might be between our two households, items each of us used only rarely.

One of the most interesting and positive trends of our modern age is the so-called sharing economy whereby people share everything from their cars to their homes. Economists, governments, and businesses don't quite know what to make of the practice of people sharing things in new ways. On the one hand, it is an incredibly practical trend that saves a great deal of money for each of us, but there is a deeper element to this trend. The sharing economy reminds us that possessing something is not a source of happiness.

As our new duplex co-owners discussed our new home, we realized that there were many things we didn't need to duplicate. We needed only one ladder, one lawn mower, one weed trimmer, and so on. I could not help but wonder how far we might take it if we were truly open to a different way of being in the world. Of course, economists might tell us that the sharing economy is bad for growth because we would need fewer cars, mowers, and ladders. The deeper question worth pondering as a society is *What made us create a system that depends on constant self-focused consumption and possession in the first place?*

redefining the good life

One of the most important conversations a society can have is how we define "the good life." In many ways our world has defined the good life as one filled with many personal possessions, as well as having many diverse experiences. This can be expressed in the concept of the gross national product, by which societal health is measured by the volume of goods we produce and use. There are consequences to that definition of a good life, even if they are unintended. A good life based on personal possessions means that we have a great deal of stuff that is used only occasionally.

Cars sit in driveways for hours on end, neighbors live next door to each other with lawn mowers that are used only once per week, houses and rooms sit empty, and snow blowers that could easily be shared take up space in every garage on the street. I hold myself up as no paragon of virtue in this regard. At one point I had one primary home and two vacation residences. The two vacation properties sat empty most of the year, partly because many other people wanted their own little piece of paradise, so there were not enough renters to fill the homes when we were not using them.

This partial use generates incredible waste, both at the front end when things are produced and at the back end when they are disposed of. The environmental costs are somewhat obvious: more toxic chemicals in the manufacturing process, more forests destroyed to create furniture and build houses, more carbon in the atmosphere, more waste-filled dump sites, and more plastic filling the oceans as our waste breaks down. The human costs are less obvious.

Everything that we possess requires that we trade something for it, usually our time. We work long and often hard hours to gather all of these possessions that rarely bring the happiness promised. Those long hours at work are often meaningful, but for many people they are not as meaningful as other things they might spend their time on, such as quality time with family and friends, volunteering, hobbies, and good works. When I gave up the two vacation homes, I could focus more on work that had meaning for me. I could turn down work that was merely taken to cover the ongoing expenses related to those homes. We could now consider my partner's retiring so that she could pursue work that was more meaningful to her.

Many millennials have eschewed possessions and spend most of their money on experiences such as travel. We don't like to admit that our experiences may be just as destructive to the planet as our possessions. Taking cruises or jet-setting around the globe to enrich our personal sense of self, or sometimes to escape the boredom of our more routine lives at home, has consequences both in terms of environmental footprint and the degradation of previously pristine natural places.

Now before you think that I am going to advocate for socialism or for building a yurt in the backyard and making vows never to travel again, let me assure you that that is not my point. Nor am I trying to heap large doses of guilt on all of us. There is nothing wrong with liking nice things, and certainly mind- (and often heart-) expanding experiences such as foreign travel have considerable merit. Yet this question of how we define the good life, both for ourselves and as a society, is a critical conversation we need to have.

The thief wants us to define the good life as getting something from outside ourselves, yet we all know somewhere deep inside that the good life has, and always will be, an internal construct. The good life lies within our own minds. We also know that relationships and love feed the soul in ways things never can.

So how do we tame the thief in society?

Here is a possible starting point: Every time I desire something outside myself, I might ask questions like *Will this bring happiness? Do I truly need this? How can I meet this need in a way that does not spread more destruction?* We can all start asking the kinds of questions that my neighbor and I did regarding our new duplex: *what can we share?* And we can extend that conversation out into our neighborhoods. When we want to have an experience or buy something that has environmental or social consequences, we can choose to confront those questions honestly rather than brush them aside. Maybe like I did with those two vacation properties, you may conclude that a different choice would make you happier and be better for the greater world.

For the broader society, we can begin by asking, *How can we create a system that brings us happiness without endless consumption being the only engine?* Decades ago futurists predicted that technology would free human beings to have more time for leisure. As we became more productive through the use of machines, we would have more time for pursuits of the heart. The opposite, of course, occurred. In developing and developed countries, most people work longer hours than ever, in part because the economic system we have created requires consumption for people to have work. The machines took over much of our work, leaving us in a faster-paced world, desperately trying to accumulate things made intentionally disposable, promising us happiness that can never be delivered.

I wish I were wise enough to know what system ought to replace the one we have created, but I'm not. Surely, the first step is to see the thief for what it is. It is lying to us about where happiness is found, and because of that our entire species works more than it must, for things we likely do not need, and in the process we are wreaking havoc on the ecosystem upon which we depend for life. A thief cannot be tamed if it is not named. So let us at least name this thief as a robber of our collective well-being and then begin new conversations about defining a good life that doesn't place consumption and possession at its center.

the yogi on the beach

Years ago while on vacation in Jamaica, I attended a daily yoga session with a wise teacher. At the end of each session, he asked us to visualize a beautiful place, either real or imagined. We were to choose a setting in which we felt calm, happy, and contented. It might be a beach, a quiet room, a temple, or a mountaintop. I chose a clearing in a forest, surrounded by large old-growth trees, with filtered sunlight warming me where I sat. Birds were singing; the sky was clear.

He asked us to go to that place and experience the deep sense of contentment we felt.

"This," he said, "is your place. It exists within you. At any moment, during any day, no matter what is going on around you, this is a place where you can go. No one has to take you there; no one has to give you permission; and when you are there, contentment is yours. Never forget: you can go to this place anytime you want, and the only one who can keep you from going there is you."

It made me think of accounts I had read of people who had survived horrific external circumstances, such as being hostages or prisoners of war. Many of them, especially those who managed to keep a sense of relative calm, wrote in one way or another about this very idea. Most of us, fortunately, will find our daily challenges to happiness far more manageable. Remember that the thief wants you to think you need something outside of yourself to choose happiness. This thief is not your friend. There is a place of contentment, and it is already within you.

four ways to banish the fourth thief

- Have a daily meditation in which you begin with the mantra, said over and over again, *I choose contentment*. Find a way to remind yourself that happiness is not *out there*.

- Whenever you find yourself saying, *I will be happy when…* or *I will be happy if…*, stop these thoughts and come back into the inner house where happiness is found. Focus on the choice to be happy now.

- Challenge the consumer in yourself. Whenever you are tempted to buy something, ask yourself if it will bring any real happiness. The thing itself is not a problem; the belief that it will bring happiness is the issue.

- In society, let's ask the deepest question: *How can we create a system that enables human livelihood but does not enslave us to things and to endless consumption that wreaks havoc on the earth.* Choose to begin treading more lightly yourself. Share things, buy less, and shed those possessions that take more value from you than they add.

mantra

I can choose happiness and contentment right now. It is a product of my mind, not a result of what is happening. Right now I will choose happiness.

chapter six

the fifth thief: comfort

The final thief—*comfort*—is an insidious one. In fact, at first glance it may even appear as a source of happiness rather than a barrier to it. This thief is like a lethargic person on the sofa, TV remote in hand. It wants us to stay on the same channel, in the same comfortable position, stuck in a routine that is not life giving. It does not care about the consequences of this routine, even if the channel we are on is no longer of interest to us or serving our higher needs.

There is a story that provides a wonderful image of what we are like when this thief is running our lives.

A man was sitting atop a large horse that was racing through a small village. The horse was running at top speed, and the man looked as though he might fall off at any moment. A stranger yelled to the man, "Where are you going?"

The man yelled back, "I don't know; ask the horse!"

When this thief is monopolizing our home, we are like that man on the horse: we find ourselves on autopilot, driven by routines and habits that may seem comfortable but simply don't serve us.

your brain and happiness

Human beings tend to love order, and our brains appear to be hardwired to make order out of chaos. We find faces in clouds, create Zodiac formations in distant constellations, and use our orderly minds on a daily basis to solve very practical problems. It is a great gift. Yet there is an irony in the nature of the human mind found in this simple paradox: our minds are hardwired for routine but excited by change.

From a neuroscientific perspective, our brains are predisposed to habit. The vast majority of our decisions are made by our subconscious brain. This is very efficient and saves energy for big or novel decisions, which are made by our conscious brain. In this way we are naturally inclined to be on autopilot as much as possible. As my friend and author Marshall Goldsmith likes to say, "Human beings are hardwired to just keep doing whatever we have been doing."

Although our brains are hardwired for routine, we are excited by change. Every time we have a new experience, meet a new person, learn something new, eat a new food, or visit a new place, we get an infusion of happy chemicals in our brain. The reason for this is simple: new information means we might have to adapt, so our brains are alert.

As the neuroscientist Alvaro Pascual-Leone once told me, "If I come around the corner and there is a lion where I did not expect one, this is important information for the future. If I come home and my wife is amorous when she normally isn't, this is important data." So our brains are kind of like a hypothesis-testing machine. New information requires us to be alert, so we get excited; the excitement tunes us in to the fact that we may learn something important for future survival. The rest of the time our brains are sort of going through the motions.

The obvious way comfort is a thief is that because our brains are excited by change, much of our happiness comes from having new experiences, facing and solving new challenges, and learning new skills. Routine is deadening to the human soul.

One of the activities I like to conduct with groups is to ask participants to identify a period of time when they felt they were most truly *alive*. I then ask them to raise their hands if this time of maximum engagement was when they were doing the same things they had been doing for some time or if it was a time when they were doing something novel, such as facing a new challenge or situation or experiencing a new place or group of people. The vast majority of people say that their most fully alive moments were times of change rather than routine.

This need to keep the fifth thief at bay plays itself out in many areas of our lives. Let's take romantic relationships as an example. Routine and comfort can kill romance. Romance comes from the unexpected. Although romance can blossom in the routine of daily living, most of us probably recall our most alive moments in intimacy as times of surprise or newness, such as a surprise weekend getaway, a novel location for lovemaking, or a special gift that broke the ordinary pattern. Novelty and happiness seem to go together.

Recent research has shown that our physical bodies and brains are also lovers of breaking out of the comfort of routine. Dementia and Alzheimer's disease have become major health issues both for families and society. Numerous studies suggest that when people continue to learn new activities, especially ones that are new and challenging, such as dancing or learning a musical instrument, the progression or onset of a loss of cognitive capacity is greatly reduced. The more we get out of our normal routines and engage our brains, the more cell growth and activity are increased.[1]

Even physical exercise is enhanced when this thief is kept at bay. For years I did the same routine on a treadmill, 30 minutes at the same speed, six times per week. I also did the exact same routines in my weight training several times a week. Frustrated with what appeared to be a lack of progress in my physical conditioning, I began researching the value of high-intensity interval training, whereby short bursts of very high-intensity workouts are followed by less intense activities. Although both steady-state and interval exercise produce benefits, emerging research suggests that the body may like variety as much as the mind does, in terms of benefits for physical conditioning and weight loss. I also found that staying with an exercise program was far easier when variety was introduced, probably because our active minds bore easily when riding the same horse day after day.[2]

getting stuck in a life pattern

There is a second, ultimately more powerful way that the fifth thief robs our happiness, both personally and collectively. Our tendency to go on autopilot, our predisposition to routine, means it is easy for us to hold on to old patterns even when they are not adaptive to our current reality. These routines or perhaps even ruts of behavior and mind-sets often lock us into patterns that get in the way of our happiness and contentment.

Here is a simple example. High school was a very difficult period in my life. Several things conspired to create an often hellish adolescence. I had terrible acne and was often teased as "zit face" by fellow students. I attended a small school, where there was literally one girl for every 24 boys, so it was hard for me to find a girlfriend. Another factor that made it challenging was that as high-school students go, I was on the intellectual side of the spectrum, but I attended a school where sports and being a "bad boy" were more valued. It was not hip to be smart, so I tried hard to excel at athletics, even though my ability was average.

I became very shy, rarely risked failure, and always tried to stay in situations where I knew I would succeed. The motto of my life became *Protect at all costs.*

By the time I got to university, my acne had cleared up. Women started taking an interest in me, and I was finally in an environment where my natural gifts of intellect were valued. On the one hand, I began to thrive, but I had fallen into a comfortable pattern of playing it safe. Reality had changed, but my internal patterns had not. Rather than risk asking out women whom I truly wanted to date, I would often ask only those I knew would say yes. Even if a relationship was not working for me, I would stay in it because of my earlier programming of staying safe. My grade-point average was great, but I avoided the toughest classes and most demanding professors to maintain my grades, as well as my self-esteem. Though I graduated with high marks and could have attended a prestigious graduate school, I chose one that fell below my aptitude, unconsciously fearing the competition of other high achievers.

The comfort and routine that were adaptive to my high-school reality were counterproductive in my young adulthood, and it has taken me years to break those patterns. My happiness, as well as my potential, were held back for some time by an old pattern of learned behavior that no longer served me.

Many of us retain patterns of adaptive behavior that helped us survive physically and emotionally but which no longer serve us. The thief holds the remote control tightly in its hand, warning us that if we change the channel, bad things will happen. Of course, the opposite is actually the case; it is only when we change the routine that once made so much sense to us to a new, more adaptive pattern that we can maximize our happiness.

Here is another example of how the thief clings to the channel changer. Perhaps you grew up in a family where conflict was avoided at all costs. When conflict was expressed, it may have given way to an eruption of verbal or physical violence. Your young mind naturally began to associate disagreement with negative consequences. You learned to stay quiet, subjugate your needs, and gloss over any potential conflict that might arise in your relationships. This pattern of behavior made sense and helped you survive your childhood home, much as my playing it safe helped me survive high school.

No one ever taught you that the willingness to raise issues and resolve them is actually conducive to healthy relationships. You never saw that by *not* talking about things, problems tend to fester and grow. You may feel resentment at glossing over your own needs just to keep the peace. You had no role model for healthy conflict resolution, so you have come to wrongly associate disagreement with bad outcomes. Now you are in a relationship, and every time there is the slightest conflict you shut down. The thief wants to keep you forever stuck in a set of habits that once made sense but now need adjustment.

Although we could continue with more examples, what might be more useful is for you to reflect on your own life. What patterns have you learned that may have been adaptive earlier in your life but no longer serve you? How is the thief keeping you hardwired to routines that are counterproductive? How can you challenge assumptions about yourself and the world?

banishing the thief

I have referenced several times the notice-stop-replace framework for banishing the thieves, so let's apply that model to our final thief. This thief may be the hardest to notice both because comfort and routine are not bad in and of themselves and also because the strong roots of the patterns that govern your life make it difficult to see them objectively.

The first step is to notice the patterns in your life that may be deeply ingrained due to your earlier experiences. For me one of those critical patterns is playing it safe by trying only those activities with which I have a great likelihood of success. There is nothing inherently wrong with that pattern, but it has often kept me from really going for what I want or daring to stretch myself. Though it is often difficult or even painful to become deeply aware of such patterns, it is critical.

As an example, a good friend of mine had a depressed father who required a great deal of caretaking from his own children. As a child my friend gladly supported his father, but this is not the normal course of things. In an ideal world, it is the parent who is emotionally available for the child rather than the child's having to support the parent. My friend says that now, as an adult, whenever someone needs him too much, it causes an overreaction on his part. Normal dependency can be seen as needy, and he will often pull back in fear of someone's demanding too much of him

Yet he is deeply cognizant of this pattern, has spent a great deal of time trying to understand it, and is hyperaware of noticing when it has him riding off on that horse on autopilot. He often tells those close to him, at work and in his personal life, about this pattern so that they can help him fight his natural tendency to withdraw just because someone needs something from him. Withdrawing from a situation is a perfectly acceptable behavior but not if it is merely the reenactment of an old pattern. By taking the time to become aware of the natural channel he is tuned to, he has been able to build healthy relationships by being supportive while maintaining healthy boundaries.

The next step is to stop. Stopping the thief doesn't always mean you will ride off in a new direction. It does mean that you won't let the horse hijack you. When I hear my inner voice saying, *Play it safe,* I have to ask myself if that voice is serving me well in that moment. When you hear that voice saying, *Conflict is bad* or *That person needs too much from me,* you need to step back and ask if this is a voice you want to heed. By being mindful, we can ask if an old pattern is serving us well in the current situation. Sometimes the answer is yes, but often it is no.

Finally, we replace the comfort thought pattern with a different one. The new filter for this thief can be summarized in this mantra:

I am not my patterns. Just because this is my habitual channel, it does not mean it serves me. I can choose a new path.

The act of being aware of a thought pattern and then replacing it with a new one can have a very practical impact on your daily life. A friend of mine is very shy by nature, due to some childhood experiences of verbal abuse. Underlying that shyness was the belief that she was never good enough in social situations and would not measure up. The behavior and underlying cause had been years in the making, so it was very hard for her to be open to people, which manifested behaviorally in a lack of eye contact, even when speaking directly to others. She became aware of this pattern, identified where and why it originated, and decided she wanted to stop the thief from stealing her ability to connect with others.

One of the decisions she made was to make a game of maintaining eye contact and not being the first to break it. Once she started doing this, it felt very uncomfortable after years of avoiding eye contact. But by making it a game, and thereby not coming from a place of judging herself, maintaining more-consistent eye contact with others came more naturally. The focus on eye contact began to break down the deeper pattern, which was the fear of openly connecting with others and of not being good enough. This is a great example of how simply stopping a habit without judgment and replacing it with a new behavior can break patterns honed over decades of life. When it comes to banishing the fifth thief, it is often best to focus on changing behavior first, so we are acting as though the new thought pattern were already dominant. The new behavior then reinforces the new thought pattern as adaptive.

The thief wants us to believe that the previous patterns of our life, and the early experiences that shaped us, become our destiny. The good news from a neuroscience perspective is that although our brains are hardwired for routine, recent research in neuroplasticity shows that old habits can be changed at any age. It just requires practicing new patterns and habits so that they replace the old ones. The first step is noticing, and then stopping and replacing. In the beginning it won't feel natural, but over time you will establish new habits that will be as robust as the ones that no longer serve you.

comfort in the world

This same thief operates at the global level. Just as the thief named comfort tricks us as individuals to keep riding a horse that is taking us in the wrong direction, so this is true for our entire species.

As a prime example, for thousands of years human beings were at the mercy of nature on a daily basis. The world was large and we were small and few. As a species we developed a pattern of seeing nature as abundant and inexhaustible. Our pattern became one in which our primary goal was to subdue nature. We learned to hunt, cultivated the land to our needs, systematically eliminated wild species with our consumption, and eventually unearthed millions of years of stored-up fuel such as oil and coal and burned them to create energy. This pattern made sense when there were a few million humans and seemingly limitless natural resources.

But just like my pattern of playing it safe served me well in high school, the patterns of comfortable routine (including how we see the world) often get in the way of society's success when reality changes. Like the man on the horse, humanity is still running in the same basic direction with the same mind-set that was established for circumstances that no longer exist.

Today there are 6.5 billion humans on the planet—4 billion more than when I was born only 58 years ago. The bountiful natural world that I was born into has changed radically in less than one human lifetime. The comfortable pattern of subduing nature as if it were unlimited once worked for us. Predisposed to routine as we are, at both the societal and personal levels, we have fished out nearly every commercial species of fish; poured tons of fertilizer into the ocean, killing the coral reefs and creating huge dead zones; dumped tons of plastic into the oceans, creating floating garbage patches hundreds of miles wide; decreased biodiversity, which is the very lifeblood of the planet, with species going extinct at a thousand times the historical average; and through carbon emissions set a course to alter the very climate upon which we depend. All of this damage has been done, in large part, not out of any evil intent but because we are still operating on an old mind-set that is no longer valid.

Surprisingly, there are still many people who believe that we as humans are much too small to change the entire planet. And they *were* right. A short time ago, there were not enough of us, nor was our technology advanced enough, to reshape the earth in a way that could endanger the future of life. Our comfortable routine of rampant consumption, uncontrolled energy use, and disregard for the role that the natural ecosystem plays in our well-being once made sense, but now that comfort threatens our very existence.

Another example is the zealous belief in free-market capitalism that exists among many people in the developed world, especially in North America. These ideologues believe that free markets are the answer to all economic and social ills. There are many merits to free-market capitalism, and certainly when compared with other systems that went before it, like communism and socialism as practiced in places like the former Soviet Union, it seems like the best of all possible systems. And it was the best system compared with totalitarian or controlled economies that limited human ingenuity.

But our fear of new ways of thinking often binds us to a system that may be working in many ways but which has led to increasing gaps between the very rich and the very poor, alongside wholesale degradation of the global environment to benefit short-term profits. Greed nearly brought down the entire world economy in 2008, and the system routinely prioritizes gross national product above the citizens' well-being. None of this is to suggest that we know the best hybrid system to replace it, but it shows how comfort with the status quo keeps us from asking the right questions. Remember that this thief wants us on that horse, thinking we are in control, when habit and routine are actually leading the way.

The same can be said of the scourge of terrorism. In a world where enemies were other nations, the mind-set that wars were won with military power and a heavy hand made complete sense. Yet reality has changed. Fighting terrorism is a war not merely of weapons but of ideas. And in the case of global terrorism, we are not fighting another nation but bands of individuals with a way of thinking that is becoming more pervasive all around the globe. Even one disgruntled person with a perverse ideology can cause devastating human losses.

The fifth thief wants us to stay tuned to the old way of thinking that worked in a world in which we no longer operate. Rather than talking about building bridges and winning the war of ideas, we spend most of our time talking about how to win with greater military, security, intelligence, and technological might. It is not that technology or the military are of no use in the war on terrorism—of course they are. The point is that we are wedded to old mind-sets that don't apply in the same way to new realities. Societies and entire nations can ride horses of habit as mindlessly as we can in our own lives.

Take, for example, the way potential terrorists are treated in most of the Western world. With the civil war in Syria and the growth of ISIS, many countries around the world are wrestling with how to deal with citizens who go to Syria with the potential to be radicalized. Most of Europe cracked down on citizens who had traveled to Syria. France shut down mosques it suspected of harboring radicals. The United Kingdom declared citizens who had gone to help ISIS enemies of the state. Several countries threatened to take away their passports.

The city of Aarhus in Denmark took a different approach starting in 2012. The local police noticed a trend of young Muslim men going to Syria. But they took an alternative tack than most of Europe. They made it clear to citizens of Denmark who had traveled to Syria that they were welcome to come home and that when they did they would receive help with schooling, finding an apartment, meeting with a psychiatrist or a mentor, or whatever they needed to fully integrate back into Danish society. Although the media dubbed the program "hug a terrorist," it is actually rooted in psychology backed by solid research.

Research shows that there is a very strong correlation between radicalization and young men being humiliated and feeling discriminated against. It also turns out that if you show warmth to people, they are most likely to respond in kind. Note that this is not about coddling terrorists, as these young men are not yet criminals. They are potential terrorists. The program has been quite successful at reintegrating these young men back into society and turning them away from radicalization.[3]

The point here is not to suggest an easy solution to a complex problem, but it does illustrate how comfort can mire us in old patterns of thinking that don't serve us. Whether personally or as entire societies, we must be aware of mind-sets that bind us to ways of thinking and acting that simply don't work.

New realities call for new solutions. What is especially important is that we take notice of the role that comfort plays in our collective responses to rapidly changing circumstances. Only by stopping the horse of habit can we begin to consider how these old patterns must adapt.

taking the reins

The fifth thief is the subtlest of all the thieves. We like comfort because it makes us feel safe and because it is efficient, but these very habits of comfort undermine the house of our happiness. It is the capacity for surprise, not routine, that brings vitality to life. It is when we take charge of the horse, grab the reins, and alter course away from habits that may have once served us that we find new ways of being in the world that truly work for us. Our entire species is riding the horse of habit to environmental devastation and a world that does not work for all. A new world is waiting, but only after we banish this thief and see it for what it is.

four ways to banish the fifth thief

- Make a commitment to try one or two new things every week. Vary your routines, from taking a new route on your daily walk to a different dating experience with your partner on a Friday night. Try new areas of learning—it is good for both your mental and physical health.

- Notice the core comfort patterns of your life. What have you carried from your past that is no longer adaptive to your life today? Identify an important pattern, and take two months to work on noticing how it shows up, then choose to ride in another direction.

- Know that you can change old habits. Challenge every habit that no longer serves you.

- In society, let's begin new conversations about how to live in harmony with nature, tame the excesses of capitalism, and think differently about how we solve our differences.

mantra

I am not my patterns. Just because this is my habitual channel, it does not mean it serves me. I can choose a new path.

chapter seven

kicking the thieves out of your house

Now that we have explored the five thieves of happiness and identified who they are, we turn to the important task of keeping them out of our life. It is helpful to think of our internal mind as a house. Because our inner mind is the home of our happiness, our main task is deciding who comes into that house. In the same way, the great task of society is to make conscious choices about what parts of our nature we will allow to rule our global house.

As bold as this is to suggest, if we can keep these five thieves from ruling our house, happiness and a deep sense of well-being are practically guaranteed. These thieves represent the major sources of suffering for us individually and collectively. Recall from the beginning of the book that the mind is the temple of our happiness. If we can rule this inner world as a benevolent and wise lord, happiness will come.

reforming the thieves

Now, of course, there is only one thing to do with thieves: throw them out of the house, right? Well, that may not be as simple as it seems. In the physical world, actual thieves are not inside you, so throwing them out is relatively straightforward: catch them, arrest them, and throw them in jail. But the problem with the thieves of happiness is that they are not outside us; they are inside.

We have been thinking of the thieves as negative thought patterns. But almost all thought patterns developed for a reason, meaning at one time or in some way they were adaptive. There are reasons to believe that each of the thieves is an outgrowth of our innate human nature.

Wanting to control things is natural to us because we have been blessed and cursed by an orderly mind that can control many things and project plans into the future. The conceit of seeing ourselves as the center of things comes naturally to us because we are born alone into the world. The tendency to compare ourselves to others and covet that which we don't have is natural because we are a very social species who learned to survive by reading the emotions of others. Our focus on consumption is deeply rooted because from our very first breath we need things outside ourselves for basic survival, such as food, water, and touch. Finally, our brains are hardwired for routine because it's a very efficient use of energy, so our tendency to seek comfort by surrendering to whatever we have been doing is inherent. Because the thieves are natural thought patterns that have been allowed to dominate, it won't be easy to completely eliminate them.

Banishing the thieves entirely would require that we eliminate parts of our self, elements that serve us well in their proper place, so what we want to do is to *reform* them, to make them submissive to our highest and wisest self, who knows that these tendencies within us, when left unchecked, rob us of the happiness and harmony that rightfully belong to us. The thieves, it turns out, are not foreign forces come to invade us; they are more like cancer cells, which are natural cells in our body that mutate and refuse to die.

But how do we reform these thieves if they are so hardwired into our way of being?

the knower

To reform the thieves, we must meet another part of our human nature: the *Knower.* Within each of us as human beings, there is a self within the self. You know that this self exists because you hear its voice frequently as you go about your day. The Knower is the part of you that is able to observe yourself, even while you are living your life. It is the part of you that smiles knowingly and says, *Ah, there you go again.*

We all experience moments when we feel we have somehow stepped outside ourselves and are now watching our own behavior. It might occur when you are frustrated about something and find yourself acting out in a way that you know is not productive. Suddenly, you realize that there is a benevolent third party observing your acting out; it says something like *Are you kidding me? Do you really think that is helping you right now?* or *Can you see yourself right now?* This is the Knower— the part of yourself that is able to observe your behavior with calm objectivity.

We don't know if any other species has this inner voice. My dog is very clever, but I don't know if he ever watches himself barking wildly when the doorbell rings and thinks to himself, *Why are you getting so worked up? You know it's never anything dangerous when the bell rings. I mean, look at yourself!* Because we are obviously made of the same matter as the other creatures with whom we share the planet, one might assume that we are not the only species with some form of this capacity. What we do know is that we as human beings have the capacity to rise above our instincts and observe the self being the self.

The five thieves are not some cosmic trick, the snake in the otherwise perfect garden. They obviously were, and are, adaptive in some important ways. It is helpful, for example, to have a mind that tries to control things, as it has led to all the advances in technology that have made human life easier and more interesting. But left unchecked by the Knower, who can see that we cannot control many things, our capacity and desire to control things becomes not a source of help but a cause of misery.

Because the Knower is the part of the self that can observe the self, it is the one who does the reforming. So the good news is that the chief reformer already lives within you. The bad news is that most of us live our lives by instinct, ignoring the Knower.

Many spiritual traditions have this notion of a Knower in some form. In Buddhism the Knower is awareness that is cosmic. This Knowing is the true nature of life; it transcends the individual and is accessible to all. When Sikhism speaks of our natural common sense, it seems to me that it is referring to the Knower. In the Christian tradition, the Holy Spirit serves that role.

So if you are a person of faith, you can think of the Knower as something that has a life of its own but is also an integral part of you, the wise self that pervades the universe. If you are a person of logic and science, you might think of the Knower as a capacity for self-reflection that is hardwired in the human mind.

No matter the context in which it is understood, it is this capacity to rise above the self to observe the self that allows us to banish the thieves. Yet many of us fail to claim this power within. We spend our days at the mercy of the thieves, when there is a self within the self that stands ready to be the wise lord of our inner temple.

Perhaps the reforming of the thieves happens most easily when we truly surrender to the Knower. The work of reforming is to gradually allow the Knower take charge of the instincts. Start listening more attentively to the part of you that recognizes the thieves, slowly allowing this inner voice to become dominant. It is the Knower who is true to us. This is the natural happiness that is already ours.

thirty days to banish the thieves

By now you probably see how each of the thieves robs us of our happiness, and you have a desire to live without them in control. But how do you do it? It is helpful to know that getting rid of these thought patterns is like developing any other habit: it takes time, discipline, and a plan.

Because few of us can commit to taking on a long-term commitment right away, I suggest a simple 30-day plan to rid your house of the thieves. It involves committing to three simple disciplines that will take no more than 15 minutes each day. The thieves may not be fully evicted after 30 days, but you will have made great strides toward training your mind for happiness.

First, commit to using the five mantras in this book by repeating them each day. I suggest beginning each day with all five mantras and then reciting them to yourself again before bedtime:

> *I choose to be in the present moment and to embrace whatever is. Happiness is not in the outcome I seek.*
>
> *I am connected to all that is; and if I can contribute to the good of the whole, happiness will find me.*

Life is not a contest. I will be grateful for what I have and who I am. I will celebrate the success of others; for when I celebrate for others, I am happy.

I can choose happiness and contentment right now. It is a product of my mind, not a result of what is happening. Right now I will choose happiness.

I am not my patterns. Just because this is my habitual channel, it does not mean it serves me. I can choose a new path.

Each day choose one of the mantras to be your main focus. For example, I might choose to focus all day on being in the present moment, stopping any worry about the future or regret about the past as soon as it begins, replacing it with the mantra. If you find yourself resisting anything that is happening that you cannot change, speak the mantra. It might be a traffic jam, the rain that canceled your golf game, or your partner not wanting to do what you want to do. Simply accept whatever is at that moment.

The second discipline is to keep a gratitude journal for 30 days. Each day identify three things that you are grateful for that day. Make the commitment and ideally do it at the same time every day, either to start your day by reflecting on the day before or at bedtime as your day ends. Then each day choose one person in your life and write down something you want to celebrate about something good happening in *their* life. This can be especially powerful if you choose something that you might envy or covet in some small way.

The third and final discipline is to spend just a few minutes every day asking, *Did any of the five thieves show up for me today?* Allow the Knower to see the pattern so that it can catch it next time. You may find that just knowing that you are going to ask yourself that question at the end of your day means you will catch yourself right when the thief shows up.

Commit to these three practices for the next 30 days. Your happiness should increase as you train your mind to welcome it.

coming down from the mountaintop

When I took eight months off to go on sabbatical, so many things became clear. I vividly recall sitting in a small coffee shop in the Andes mountains of Peru and writing down the clear truths from my journey, including the names of the five thieves. But as the great mythologist Joseph Campbell once noted, the hero's journey is never complete until you come back to the real world and put into practice what you have learned.[1]

So you might rightly wonder if I found the happiness I sought.

The biggest shift for me since my time disconnecting from my normal life has been the realization that contentment is fostered in the discipline of daily practice. For years I sought happiness in the way many people seek it. I spent my life trying to get the "happenings" of my life to be just perfect so that I could be happy. The greatest realization has been that true lasting contentment comes from training the mind and heart for happiness.

Few of us will ever be happy all the time. The Buddha saw it clearly. Suffering in the external world is always present and can be transformed only by wisdom. Wisdom is to see things clearly. I am much happier than when I began this journey. Like the Buddha, I feel more awake.

The thieves are still lurking, but their capacity to trick me has greatly diminished. There is a poem by David Whyte titled "Statue of Buddha." It says, "faithful to all things as you met them, until everything bowed to you."[2] It is precisely because the Buddha bowed to everything by embracing whatever was in an awake state that eventually everything bowed to him. The journey to happiness is ultimately a daily walk to encounter all things as they come to you, including the thieves. If we are willing to stay faithful to our practice, the thieves will eventually bow to us.

chapter eight

imagining a world without the five thieves

Throughout this book, we have discussed the role that the five thieves play, not only in our personal lives but in our community life as well, as humanity as a whole is an extension of each individual's personal house. In my years of consulting with organizations, this has become apparent to me again and again. An organization is not an entity but rather the sum of its parts. A society does not exist in the truest sense because we cannot feel or touch it. What we call society is the web of interactions of many individuals that over time establishes a set of norms for how we act, but the source of those behavioral norms is the individuals within the society. Because of this, all societal or organizational change must begin as personal change.

Otto Scharmer at the MIT Sloan School of Management likes to quote a CEO he interviewed years ago, who said, "The quality of the initiative is in direct proportion to the inner life of the initiator." This is another way of saying that the organization is an extension of the inner life of those who lead it. Of course, this is not always welcome news because we would prefer to blame society or the organization for whatever is not working, rather than look at the way our inner life might be changing the world around us.

In my previous book, *Stepping Up: How Taking Responsibility Changes Everything,* I explored this idea more fully. Suffice it to say that finger pointing has become endemic across the world and certainly in Western society. Everyone acts as though someone else has created the problems that plague society, instead of looking at the way society is an outgrowth of our own inner house. We want a different world without looking deeply into our own self. That is why there are two reasons to reform the thieves within; the first is selfish and the second altruistic. We must tame the thieves to be happy; but we must also reform them within ourselves because until we do, the world will not change.

A simple example may help. If we explore the divisive political environment in the United States, our first instinct is to blame the politicians and perhaps the media for this obviously dysfunctional climate. Yet closer inspection shows that the whole society finds it difficult to talk about differences of opinion. The first thief, control, permeates society, wanting us to shield ourselves from the cognitive dissonance of views divergent from our own. The common adage that it is best to avoid talking about politics and religion is a truism not because the politicians are divided. It is our own inability to put aside control long enough to actually listen to those who don't share our views. That is why cleaning up our own house is always the first step.

Mahatma Gandhi said, "The only devils in this world are those running around in our own hearts, and that is where all our battles should be fought."[1]

It is likely why Jesus said, "First take the log out of your own eye, and then you will see clearly to take out the speck that is in your brother's eye."[2]

All the great teachers call on us to look within for the evils we want to root out of the world.

Individual transformation is critical. For *Stepping Up* we surveyed people to find out why they don't step up more to try to change the world. The number one answer was that people felt that because they were only one person, they would not have much influence. In the task of ridding the thieves from our collective world, however, one person matters a great deal. One person creates a ripple that changes their small circle: family, friends, children, and co-workers. One person matters because ultimately all significant change is the result of millions of individuals making a shift. Society does not shift; people do.

thieves running wild in the world

Currently, the five thieves are running wild in the world. The Knower is not in charge of our collective house. Yet there is a part of us as a species that can rise above the noise to see, without judgment, what is really going on.

The first thief, control, has people all over the world holding on to their own views instead of exploring creative solutions to the problems we face. Because we have such a need to believe that our views are the correct views, a likely outgrowth of realizing that we are not truly in control of so many things, we are unable to work together to discover common ground.

The second thief, conceit, has each one of us acting as though the world revolves around us, which by extension means "my generation." In other words, as we look mostly to our own ego for satisfaction, we fail to see that this generation and its own needs matter little in the big scheme of things. The great experiment of life began long before our generation, and we have the privilege of being part of it. This thief has driven us to use the world's bounty in one generation to the detriment of not only future generations but of life itself. Only when we reform the thief and truly see that meaning comes from our contribution to the call of life itself will humanity be a force for evolutionary good.

The third thief, coveting, creates a world in which we believe that some must lose for me to win. After all, someone must be the fairest of them all, the richest of them all, and the most famous of them all. Coveting drives us to see others as an impediment to our own happiness, and that sows the seeds of violence, genocide, and the wrongheaded idea that everyone cannot win. We must redefine winning away from me-against-you and toward a world where everyone thrives, not only because it is fair but because it will help us survive.

The fourth thief, consumption, has tricked us into creating a world in which we consume more and more as a means to happiness. Happiness, of course, cannot be found in things but is a choice available to us at each moment. Our current economic system is not focused on collective well-being but instead requires destructive consumption for people to make a living. Our desire for more things means a life cluttered with possessions but sorely lacking in community and meaning. This thief tricks us into measuring well-being by how much we consume instead of the experience of shared happiness.

The fifth thief, comfort, keeps humanity wedded to habits that no longer serve us, such as tribalism and seeing nature as something to subdue. Both of these worldviews were somewhat adaptive, or at least nonfatal, in a time of smaller, more local societies. But in the world of the twenty-first century, focusing on the good of my tribe and seeing nature as something only to exploit promises only to leave us with an environmentally decimated planet where inequality threatens to cause more and more civil instability, both within and between countries.

a world without the thieves

Of course it is an oversimplification to blame all the ills of the world on the thieves, but if we were to imagine a world with these thieves gone, we can begin to see the possibilities.

Think for a moment about the John Lennon song "Imagine," which strikes a chord of deep resonance across so many cultures. Why is such a simple lyric sung by so many in such a variety of languages?

"Imagine" posits a world without the thieves. It is a world with no country and no religion, nothing to live or die for. It is a world in which there are no possessions. It is a world in which we are living for today, deeply here in the present moment. In a few short lyrics, Lennon imagined a world where control, conceit, coveting, consumption, and comfort were all tamed.

As a young person who was very religious, I found Lennon's line "no religion" somewhat offensive. But now with some wisdom of age on my side, it is obvious to me that it was not a lack of religion or spirituality that he imagined to be so healing. It was a world in which religion was not a source of division because of our need to control the views of others.

It is unfair to say that religion is the cause of the ills of the world, as some have posited. An objective view of human history would likely lead to the conclusion that religion has been a force for both good and evil. Many of the noblest ideas of humanity have come from its many religions, but even religions can be infected with the thieves.

When religion or any belief system is ruled by thieves, it becomes a destructive force. A religion that seeks to control others, that is conceited enough to see itself as the only truth or sees humans as the only spirited life, that covets by positing that only it is the fairest truth of all, that sees consumption of dogma as the source of redemption rather than the perfecting of

the human mind, and that is ruled by comfort and an unwilling-
ness to adapt—such a religion will not serve humanity's future.
Fortunately, there have always been prophets in every faith to
call it back to its noble truths.

a mindful society

To tame the thieves in our collective world, we must be willing
to practice the same mindfulness as a society that is required of
us as individuals. Using the same simple idea—notice, stop, and
replace—we can begin to reimagine a different world. The main
task for each of us, of course, is to catch, arrest, and reform the
thieves within ourselves; by so doing we will become a different
kind of citizen in the world. No longer ruled by thieves, we will
act in a way that builds the world that we want to create.

There is a role for the five thieves, however, as a conscious
frame in which to see collective life. Because I have spent most
of my life in the world of large businesses, let me use that realm
as an example.

Most large businesses are ruled by the thieves to the detriment of both their own entity and the communities in which
they operate. For example, conceit leads a company to think
that the world revolves around it, rather than the other way
around. Businesses thrive when the context in which they work
thrives. I heard an executive at Coca-Cola, talking about the
company's efforts in sustainability and social responsibility, put
it this way: "We have had a 120-year run, and we want another
120-year run. But if society does not thrive, people will not buy
our products, and we will not thrive." In other words, he was
recognizing that conceit would not serve his company well.

Businesses must see that unless they aid in solving the great
problems of our day, such as inequality, intolerance, and sustainability, there is no thriving future for them. They are connected

to the health of the places they do business in, not the other way around.

What is sorely needed are companies and leaders who see that only by focusing on the health of the whole world can business thrive. A myopic focus on their own survival at the cost of the greater good will serve them for only a short time.

Coveting might temporarily blind them to this truth, as they listen to the mirror of quarterly profits telling them, "You are the most profitable of them all." But the comparison will blind them to the many ways that cooperating with others will ensure their long-term survival. An agricultural company may maximize profits in the short term by using unsustainable practices, but, in the long run, only by creating standards for sustainable practices will the entire industry survive.

The same is true for governments and nations. In the short term, a conceited focus on our own tribal needs might appear to be in our self-interest. But everyone focusing on their own self-interest likely means growing inequality. Inequality and poverty foster instability. Instability often leads to repressive governments and radicalization of citizens. Soon we all will need to live in a world of gated nations, but like gated communities sitting amid poverty, eventually the gates will not be high enough to keep the problems from hitting home. A world that works for all will ultimately work for every individual part.

Once we are aware of the thieves, we will see the many ways they affect society. We must begin by stepping back and noticing what is already happening around us.

The same three steps apply: we notice the thieves, with nonjudgment we stop them when they do not serve us, and we choose another path. This will not be easy, but there are signs around the globe of an emerging Knower consciousness—humanity's ability to look at our own behavior, stepping back mindfully to take a divergent path—that may build the world we hope to live in.

It is this very capacity for rising above the experience of the moment that is most required for humanity at this moment in time. The spiritual traditions discovered the power of mindfulness and meditation over several millennia, but only now are we beginning to see that this ability to rise above experience and observe it might be the very skill most needed for humanity's evolution. Only then can we collectively observe the way the thieves are robbing our species of our highest potential.

In a world where the thieves are banished, we could do the following:

- Cease our desire to control others to make them see the world as we do and instead create space for true dialogue and understanding among religions and worldviews

- Define happiness by the well-being of the whole society and even the planet

- Tame the coveting spirit that allows us to see others as obstacles to our happiness and create a win-win world

- Challenge a system built upon endless consumption that has fostered loneliness rather than happiness

- Challenge the habits of our species that no longer serve us well, such as tribalism and seeing nature as here only for our use

claiming our true nature

This book began with a simple premise and will end in that same place. Happiness is our natural state. We are born deeply connected to all life, so much so that life can come only from other life. Separation is an illusion. The child, so long as he or she is fed and loved, will naturally smile back at the world. If we tame the thieves, we will find the happiness that is rightfully ours.

Humans are a cooperative, generous, and ultimately constructive force for the future of evolution. We became so successful as a species precisely because we learned to cooperate and work together. Now we must reform the thieves to leave our narrow tribalism behind—our conceit of wanting the world to be about us—and use our creativity to improve life on earth for ourselves and all other living things.

There is great reason to be optimistic about our species in spite of all the negative events that fill the news. As my nearly 30-year-old daughter likes to say, "We know the good is winning; after all, we are here." It was our compassion and capacity to cooperate that allowed us to thrive this long. The darker side is there and cannot be denied, but the true nature underneath this, us without the thieves, is who we are.

The temple of happiness for ourselves and our species is in our minds. We must allow the Knower to rise above the noise, notice the thieves for who they are, stop their unlimited reign, and choose a new path. Not only can we do this, but collectively we must.

notes

chapter one   happiness is our natural state

1. Tamlin S. Conner and Katie A. Reid, "Effects of Intensive Mobile Happiness Reporting in Daily Life," *Social Psychological and Personality Science* 3, no. 3 (2012): 315–23. doi: 10.1177 /1948550611419677.

2. For a more extensive review of the cooperative nature of *Homo sapiens,* read these two books: Edward O. Wilson, *The Social Conquest of Earth* (New York: Liveright, 2013); and Yuval Noah Harari, *Sapiens: A Brief History of Humankind* (New York: HarperCollins, 2014).

3. In addition to Harari's book *Sapiens,* take a look at this article on hunter-gatherer tribes as caregivers, which suggests that we might even learn some important things about parenting from our ancient ancestors: Danielle Friedman, "Parent Like a Caveman," The Daily Beast, October 10, 2010, http://www .thedailybeast.com/articles/2010/10/11/hunter-gatherer -parents-better-than-todays-moms-and-dads.html.

chapter two   the first thief: control

1. The collective biographical information about Siddhārtha Gautama is from several sources but primarily Universal Theosophy, accessed August 28, 2016, http://www.universal theosophy.com/buddha-the-life-of-siddhartha-gautama.

2. Luke 12:25 (New International Version).

3. *Merriam-Webster Dictionary,* online ed., s.v. "mindfulness," accessed August 3, 2016, http://www.merriam-webster.com/dic tionary/mindfulness.

4. Wikipedia, s.v. "Mind monkey," last modified June 10, 2016, https://en.wikipedia.org/wiki/Mind_monkey.

5. Geoffrey Skelley, "Reviewing the Convention Ratings," Sabato's Crystal Ball, September 13, 2012, http://www.centerforpolitics .org/crystalball/articles/reviewing-the-convention-ratings.

chapter three   the second thief: conceit

1. Kathryn Buchanan and Anat Bardi, "Acts of Kindness and Acts of Novelty Affect Life Satisfaction," *The Journal of Social Psychology* 150, no. 3 (2010): 235–37. doi: 10.1080/00224540903365554.

2. For more on the Gaia hypothesis, see http://www.gaiatheory.org /overview.

3. For a full rendering of this hypothesis, read Yuval Noah Harari's wonderful book *Sapiens: A Brief History of Human Kind* (New York: HarperCollins, 2014).

4. To learn more about Hadza, this article offers a great overview: Michael Finkel, "The Hadza," *National Geographic*, December 2009, http://ngm.nationalgeographic.com/2009/12/hadza /finkel-text.

chapter four   the third thief: coveting

1. Exodus 20:17 (New International Version).

2. Katherine A. De Cellas and Michael I. Norton, "Physical and Situational Inequality on Airplanes Predicts Air Rage," *Proceedings of National Academy of Sciences* 113, no. 20 (2016): 5588–91. doi: 10.1073/pnas.1521727113.

3. Richard Wilkinson and Kate Pickett, *The Spirit Level: Why Greater Equality Makes Societies Stronger* (New York: Bloomsbury Press, 2009).

4. Robert Emmons and his colleagues have published scores of articles on gratitude. For a great summary of his work, see Robert A. Emmons "Why Gratitude Is Good," DailyGood, June 20,

2011, http://www.dailygood.org/story/8/why-gratitude-is-good
-robert-a-emmons.

5. Ann Morin, "7 Scientifically Proven Benefits of Gratitude,"
Psychology Today, April 3, 2016, https://www.psychologytoday
.com/blog/what-mentally-strong-people-dont-do/201504/7
-scientifically-proven-benefits-gratitude.

6. Olivia Blair, "Staying off Facebook Can Make You Happier,
Study Claims," *Independent,* November 10, 2015, http://
www.independent.co.uk/life-style/gadgets-and-tech/news
/staying-off-facebook-can-make-you-happier-study-claims
-a6728056.html.

7. Maria Konnikova, "How Facebook Makes Us Unhappy," *The
New Yorker,* September 10, 2013, http://www.newyorker.com
/tech/elements/how-facebook-makes-us-unhappy.

8. Moira Burke, Cameron Marlow, and Thomas Lento, "Social
Network Activity and Social Well-Being," *CHI 2010:
Proceedings of the SIGCHI Conference on Human Factors in
Computing Systems,* April 10–15, 2010, 1909–12. doi: 10.1145
/1753326.1753613.

9. "Bob Newhart—Stop It," published March 12, 2015, https://
www.youtube.com/watch?v=arPCE3zDRg4.

chapter five   **the fourth thief: consumption**

1. William Shakespeare, *The Tragedy of Hamlet, Prince of Denmark,*
act 2, sc. 2, accessed August 8, 2016, http://shakespeare.mit
.edu/hamlet/hamlet.2.2.html.

2. Joseph P. Forgas, "Four Ways Sadness May Be Good for You,"
Greater Good Science Center, June 4, 2014, http://greater
good.berkeley.edu/article/item/four_ways_sadness_may_be
_good_for_you.

chapter six   **the fifth thief: comfort**

1. "The Search for Alzheimer's Prevention Strategies," National Institute on Aging website, accessed August 3, 2016, https://www .nia.nih.gov/alzheimers/publication/preventing-alzheimers -disease/search-alzheimers-prevention-strategies.

2. For a somewhat exhaustive review of research on interval versus steady-state exercise routines, see Micah Zuhl, PhD, and Len Kravitz, PhD, "HIIT vs Continuous Endurance Training: Battle of the Aerobic Titans," University of New Mexico website, accessed August 3, 2016, https://www.unm.edu/~lkravitz /Article%20folder/HIITvsCardio.html.

3. Hanna Rosin, "How a Danish Town Helped Young Muslims Turn Away from ISIS," Jefferson Public Radio, July 15, 2016, http:// www.npr.org/sections/health-shots/2016/07/15/485900076 /how-a-danish-town-helped-young-muslims-turn-away-from -isis.

chapter seven   **kicking the thieves out of your house**

1. See Joseph Campbell, *The Hero with a Thousand Faces* (Novato, CA: New World Library, 2008).

2. David Whyte, "Statue of Buddha," in *River Flow: New and Selected Poems,* rev. ed. (Langley, WA: Many Rivers Press, 2012): 308

chapter eight   **imagining a world without the five thieves**

1. Dr. Purushothaman, *Words of Wisdom: 1001 Quotes & Quotations,* vol. 44 (Kollam, Kerala, India: Center for Human Perfection, 2014), 93.

2. Luke 6:42 (English Standard Version).

acknowledgments

Over the past two decades, I have written six other books, and so many of the people who helped me have been constant over those years. Yet I am always grateful that there are new helpers who show up with each endeavor.

Thanks to Steve Piersanti and the amazing team at Berrett-Koehler. This is my fourth book with them, and their dedication to bringing important ideas to the world continues to inspire me. Steve always helps me take my ideas and make them better. Thanks for your ongoing belief in my work.

Thanks to my life partner, Janice Halls. She remains the most deeply spiritual person I know, and much of what I write about in this book she role-models for me every day. She helps keep the thieves out of our house. My gratitude for your presence grows every year.

Thanks to my friends and colleagues at the Learning Network, who always support and challenge me. Although most of them are writers themselves, they never fail to step up to help in all ways possible. Special thanks go to my friend Marshall Goldsmith. He is one of those people who, when you ask him to help, responds only with "What do you need and by when?" Your work and your generosity continue to inspire me.

Thanks to my mother for her ongoing love and support. Even in her eighties she reads voraciously, so it is no wonder the writing bug bit me. No matter what I have tried to do in my life, she has always been my biggest cheerleader.

Thanks to the friends who encouraged me to take a sabbatical to explore a deeper happiness for myself. Among them I want to thank Chris Cappy and David Kuhl in particular. Many friends had walked the Camino and encouraged me to do the same. This book would not have been born without that walk.

Thanks to the great team at Speaker's Spotlight, who continue to promote my work as a speaker to the world. I couldn't ask for better partners, and I look forward to our helping thousands of people find more happiness while building a better world for all.

Thanks to my many friends, new and old, who fill my life with so much joy. You know who you are, and I would not want to leave anyone out. Special thanks always to my brother of another mother, Jeremy Ball. We have walked many years together to help awaken the soul, and I hope we will do so for many more.

Thanks to KoAnn Skrzyniarz and her organization, Sustainable Brands. You are at the forefront of redefining the good life, and your courage to lead conversations that make a difference helped embolden me to make this book about more than personal happiness.

Thanks to all the travelers I met during my sabbatical, especially the fellow pilgrims on the Camino. A special thanks to Jim, an American I met on the walk, who told me the next book would come but to make sure it was divinely inspired. We spent only a few hours together, but it made a big difference for me.

Thanks to Linda in my office, who keeps my life sane and helps with all things work related.

Thanks to Gary Bello and Duncan Shields, whose strong voices helped me navigate a challenging time to find a deeper well of happiness.

Thanks to the thousands of people who have shared their stories with me for all these years. Much of what I know has come from listening.

Finally, thanks to my mentor and friend, John Mroz. He left this world way too soon but showed me the power of purpose by his life example. When I asked you to walk with me on the Camino, even though you had already left this world, even then you did not disappoint me.

index

acceptance, 34–35

adaptive behavior, 97

adaptive routines, 97

air rage, 63

ambition, 77

antisocial behavior, 63

Aristotle, 2–3

assessment of happiness, 2

attachment to outcomes, 14–15.
  See also letting go

attention, compared with
  attachment, 13–15

awake, sense of being, 24–25

awareness
  act of, 100
  of control, 35
  of eternal and connected
    nature, 41
  of inner thoughts, 25–26,
    85–86, 99
  of larger truths, 45
  practicing, 28–29
  of the thieves, 32, 71–72,
    121
  See also the Knower;
    mindfulness

banishing the thieves
  gaining wisdom for, 113–114
  meeting the Knower,
    109–111
  notice step for, 20, 26–28,
    35, 120
  reforming the thieves,
    108–109

replace step for, 27–28, 35,
  45, 73, 85, 98, 100, 103,
  120

steps in, 24–26

stop step for, 23, 27–28,
  35–45, 72, 75, 91, 105,
  112, 120

30-day plan for, 110–113

30-day commitment to,
  111–113

See also mantras for banishing
  the thieves *or under
  specific thief, e.g.* comfort
  (fifth thief)

behavior(s)
  adaptive, 97
  antisocial, 63
  changing, 100–101
  effects of coveting on, 75–76
  ethical, 74
  humanity's, 121–122
  patterns of, 98
  prosocial, 64
  stopping an act/thought,
    72–73
  watching our own, 109

beliefs. *See* worldview/belief
  systems

Benyus, Janine, 42

best self, 77

Bible, 32–33, 47

brain, 94, 95, 108

Buddhism/Buddha
  Buddha's search for
    enlightenment, 39–40
  five hindrances in, 7, 10
  hungry ghost concept, 80

about the author

John Izzo has been a minister, an acclaimed speaker, a journalist, an executive coach, and a community leader. He is the best-selling author of six previous books including *Awakening Corporate Soul, Stepping Up,* and *The Five Secrets You Must Discover before You Die.*

He is a sought-after keynote speaker at both conferences and corporate events, having spoken to more than 1 million people globally. His client list reads like a who's who of business, including IBM, Qantas, the Mayo Clinic, Humana, Microsoft, Hewlett-Packard, TELUS, Walmart, and McDonald's. Each year he speaks at more than 70 conferences and frequently leads retreats on personal leadership effectiveness.

Izzo's book *The Five Secrets You Must Discover before You Die* was the basis of a successful five-hour television program that was produced by the Biography Channel and later aired on PBS. The book, for which he interviewed 250 people ages 60 to 106, asking them to reflect back on what they had learned about life, has been translated into more than 20 languages.

He was a pioneer in the corporate social responsibility movement and is involved extensively in helping create a more sustainable future. Beyond his work as a speaker and an author, he has been involved extensively in efforts for conservation and for creating a more sustainable future. He is co-founder of The Men's Initiative, affiliated with the University of British

Columbia, dedicated to building a sustainable future through enhancing the integrity and well-being of men globally.

Izzo holds master's degrees in psychology and theology, as well as a doctorate in communication studies. He has served on the faculties at two major universities.

He makes his home in Vancouver, Canada, and in Rancho Mirage, California.

contacting dr. izzo

To contact the author or to book a speaking engagement, e-mail john@drjohnizzo.com.

visit his website

www.drjohnizzo.com

follow him on twitter

@DrJohnIzzo

Also by John Izzo, PhD

The Five Secrets You Must Discover Before You Die

Based on a highly acclaimed public television series, this inspiring book reveals the keys to lasting happiness gleaned from the author's interviews with more than 200 people, ages 60 to 106, who were identified by friends and acquaintances as "the one person they knew who had found happiness and meaning." From town barbers to Holocaust survivors, from aboriginal chiefs to CEOs, they answered questions like, What brought you the greatest joy? What do you wish you had learned sooner? What ultimately mattered and what didn't? Here Izzo shares their stories—funny, moving, and thought-provoking—and the Five Secrets they revealed. This book will make you laugh, move you to tears, and inspire you to discover what matters long before you die.

Paperback, 200 pages, ISBN 978-1-57675-475-7
PDF ebook, ISBN 978-1-57675-551-8
ePub ISBN 978-1-60509-531-8

BK® Berrett–Koehler Publishers, Inc.
www.bkconnection.com   **800.929.2929**

Stepping Up
How Taking Responsibility Changes Everything

Izzo gives readers the key to a great career, a great workplace, better relationships, and a better world. *Stepping Up* argues that almost every problem, from personal difficulties and business challenges to social issues, can be solved if all of us look to ourselves to create change rather than looking to others. He offers seven compelling principles that enable anyone, anywhere, anytime to effectively bring about positive change.

Paperback, 184 pages, ISBN 978-1-60994-057-7
PDF ebook ISBN 978-1-60994-058-4
ePub ebook ISBN 978-1-60994-059-1

Second Innocence
Rediscovering Joy and Wonder

Drawing on on his own experiences—the death of his father, a rowing trip with his grandfather, his first real job, his first love, a family suicide, and his experiences as a leader, lover, parent, and friend—Izzo encourages you to reconnect with and learn from your own life stories and reclaim the innocence, idealism, and wonder that we often associate with youth.

Paperback, 208 pages, ISBN 978-1-57675-263-0
PDF ebook, ISBN 978-1-60509-282-9
ePub ebook ISBN 978-1-60994-386-8

BK Berrett–Koehler Publishers, Inc.
www.bkconnection.com   **800.929.2929**

Berrett–Koehler
Publishers

Berrett-Koehler is an independent publisher dedicated to an ambitious mission: *connecting people and ideas to create a world that works for all*.

We believe that to truly create a better world, action is needed at all levels—individual, organizational, and societal. At the individual level, our publications help people align their lives with their values and with their aspirations for a better world. At the organizational level, our publications promote progressive leadership and management practices, socially responsible approaches to business, and humane and effective organizations. At the societal level, our publications advance social and economic justice, shared prosperity, sustainability, and new solutions to national and global issues.

A major theme of our publications is "Opening Up New Space." Berrett-Koehler titles challenge conventional thinking, introduce new ideas, and foster positive change. Their common quest is changing the underlying beliefs, mindsets, institutions, and structures that keep generating the same cycles of problems, no matter who our leaders are or what improvement programs we adopt.

We strive to practice what we preach—to operate our publishing company in line with the ideas in our books. At the core of our approach is stewardship, which we define as a deep sense of responsibility to administer the company for the benefit of all of our "stakeholder" groups: authors, customers, employees, investors, service providers, and the communities and environment around us.

We are grateful to the thousands of readers, authors, and other friends of the company who consider themselves to be part of the "BK Community." We hope that you, too, will join us in our mission.

A BK Life Book

This book is part of our BK Life series. BK Life books change people's lives. They help individuals improve their lives in ways that are beneficial for the families, organizations, communities, nations, and world in which they live and work. To find out more, visit **www.bk-life.com**.

Berrett–Koehler
Publishers

Connecting people and ideas
to create a world that works for all

Dear Reader,

Thank you for picking up this book and joining our worldwide community of Berrett-Koehler readers. We share ideas that bring positive change into people's lives, organizations, and society.

To welcome you, we'd like to offer you a free e-book. You can pick from among twelve of our bestselling books by entering the promotional code **BKP92E** here: http://www.bkconnection.com/welcome.

When you claim your free e-book, we'll also send you a copy of our e-newsletter, the *BK Communiqué*. Although you're free to unsubscribe, there are many benefits to sticking around. In every issue of our newsletter you'll find

- A free e-book
- Tips from famous authors
- Discounts on spotlight titles
- Hilarious insider publishing news
- A chance to win a prize for answering a riddle

Best of all, our readers tell us, "Your newsletter is the only one I actually read." So claim your gift today, and please stay in touch!

Sincerely,

Charlotte Ashlock
Steward of the BK Website

Questions? Comments? Contact me at bkcommunity@bkpub.com.

Certified

Corporation
bcorporation.net